WE ARE WHAT WE SPEAK

Retreat Leader Guide

WORKBOOK

RICHARD T. CASE

To my wife, Linda, who has always understood and lived out the truth

that what we speak both reflects our true hearts

and provides power to our situations and circumstances of our lives.

She illustrates in her everyday life how we are to live in oneness with Him

and overcome the struggle of the heart—the flesh vs. the Spirit.

We are to abide in the Vine, spending time with Him to receive His heart

which then becomes our heart—which then teaches us what not to speak

and then what we are to speak. She has learned how we are to speak

as prophets and exercise God's authority into our circumstances

and other's circumstances. She reminds us we are to pay attention to what

we say, and that our words have meaning and power.

We work together on having the heart of the Spirit and being able to

speak His words, and His heart in our conversations, dialogues,

and discussing our circumstances. What a joy to have her live this out

and keep us in the center of this essential truth of life.

She always lives in joy, and thus brings true joy to me

as we walk with God together.

An honor to experience this together, honey!

Acknowledgments

We wish to thank all of the leaders of our **Ministry: Living Waters—ABIDE Ministries!** These leaders daily and faithfully also are learning to become One with God as they speak the truth that is in their hearts—and together are always giving this away to others who are being called by God to live in this power. Thank you all.

These leaders are:

Jake and Mary Beckel
Heath and Rebecca Cardie
Rich and Janet Cocchiaro
Larry and Sherry Collet
David and Melissa Dunkel
Tom and Susanne Ewing
Rick and Kelly Ferris
Joel and Christina Gunn
Brad and Latisha Hawkins
Rick and Nancy Hoover
Don and Rachelle Light
Steve and Carolyn Van Ooteghem
Preston and Lynda Pitts
Dan and Kathy Rocconi
Bob and Keri Rockwell
Allyson and Denny Weinberg

WE ARE WHAT WE SPEAK WORKBOOK
ABIDE MINISTRIES
7615 Lemon Gulch Way
Castle Rock, CO 80108

ISBN: 979-8-218-33235-8

Printed in the United States of America 2025 — 1st ed

TABLE OF CONTENTS

INTRODUCTION

Welcome to our course, *We Are What We Speak*. This is a very exciting course, particularly in today's time and especially because of the conversations going on in the Christian world and with unbelievers. We have drifted into a very negative place. Our world has gone crazy with all of the uncertainty, dramatic changes, and increased trouble. Circumstances are tough. They're complicated. Nothing's easy or simple. At this moment, which is post COVID, the world is having what's called "supply chain issues," and there are things that you just can't get or things that will take a while to get no matter how desperately you might need them. The world is hard and complicated, and when it moves toward the negative, we tend to talk negatively to each other. We further tend to talk negatively to ourselves. In this course, we are going to discuss the importance of understanding how to deal with that—and the impact of what we speak.

> "God tells us we are to learn to speak based upon His leading—His opening up doors for us to speak. He further describes that our speech is to be done with grace, seasoned with the flavor of positivity."

Read Colossians 4:2–6:

Further Instructions
[2] Continue steadfastly in prayer, being watchful in it with thanksgiving. [3] At the same time, pray also for us, that God may open to us a door for the word, to declare the mystery of Christ, on account of which I am in prison— [4] that I may make it clear, which is how I ought to speak.

If you'd like to know more about
Abide Ministries,
please see our pages
at the back of the workbook

INTRODUCTION

> [5] Walk in wisdom toward outsiders, making the best use of the time. [6] Let your speech always be gracious, seasoned with salt, so that you may know how you ought to answer each person.

God tells us we are to learn to speak based upon His leading—His opening up doors for us to speak. He further describes that our speech is to be done with grace, seasoned with the flavor of positivity. We then need to know how to respond to others as they react to our conversation.

There are a number of significant questions for each of us regarding how we speak: How do you typically speak to your spouse and friends? Are you negative? Are you harsh? Are you judgmental? How about your small group? It may not be what you speak of to your small group, rather what you speak about your small group. What about how you speak to people who hurt, disagree, or disappoint you—especially given the fact that this will continue to happen? How about others who aren't like you or don't hold any of the same beliefs that you have? For example, in the political world, we know today in America, there are two main parties, Democrats and Republicans. How well do they talk to each other? Currently, neither party has any concern about what the other party thinks. Instead, they go after each other after you, oftentimes viciously.

If someone says something you don't believe, how do you respond? Do you try to silence them with your words? Given that we live in a cancel culture, you try to cancel the person who believes differently. The enemy brings about division because, as we know, a house divided cannot stand. Division, canceling, negativity, hateful words are goals of the enemy.

Further, this affects how you speak to yourself. How do you talk to yourself? What do you think of yourself? Most people are pretty disappointed because they think God's not that happy with them. Because of this, you speak things to yourself in ways that represent that disappointment, *You're not good enough. You are an idiot. You are a fool.* Unfortunately, you're speaking these words into your very own soul. So, how do we end the negative talk in this very tough world? How do we live that out?

Write down in your workbook or journal: What are the issues, situations, circumstances, or decisions that you're seeking resolution or favorable outcome?

This course will help you understand how you speak to yourself and others who are in different relationships with you—both positive and negative friendships, those who oppose you, your spouse or partner, family members, believers, and unbelievers—and how to process with each. It's not you speaking holy theology and doing things correctly—rather it is how are you acting and reacting in real-life situations. This response will be made clear by how you speak about and process each of these circumstances.

LESSON 1: GOD'S PURPOSE—LIVE IN ONENESS WITH HIM; OUR SPEAKING REFLECTS OUR HEART, WHICH IS IN A STRUGGLE BETWEEN THE FLESH AND THE SPIRIT.

What is the purpose for which Christ has come? When is this available to us? What does that mean for how we are to live? Why?

Read John 10:10:

10 The thief comes only to steal and kill and destroy. I came that they may have life and have it abundantly.

____

____

____

____

____

"God's purpose right now is to give you a super-abundant life."

God's purpose right now is to give you a super-abundant life. We know there is an enemy, a thief, who will do whatever he can to thwart God's purpose for you. Our receiving God's super-abundant life is not done in a bubble where trouble from the enemy is absent. It is in the middle of that, and it is absolute. He has come to give us life and give it to us super-abundantly. He describes this in more detail in Isaiah.

This is Christ's first public statement of His ministry when He read these verses in the synagogue in Nazareth and stated that He was the fulfillment of this for all of us. What specifically did He say were the things that define the super-abundant life He has come to give us? What do they mean to us, and what we can thus expect?

Read Isaiah 61:1–4:

The Year of the LORD'S Favor

61 The Spirit of the LORD GOD is upon me,
   because the LORD has anointed me
to bring good news to the poor;[a]
   he has sent me to bind up the brokenhearted,
to proclaim liberty to the captives,
   and the opening of the prison to those who are bound;[b]
2 to proclaim the year of the LORD'S favor,
   and the day of vengeance of our God;
   to comfort all who mourn;
3 to grant to those who mourn in Zion—
   to give them a beautiful headdress instead of ashes,
the oil of gladness instead of mourning,
   the garment of praise instead of a faint spirit;
that they may be called oaks of righteousness,
   the planting of the LORD, that he may be glorified.[c]
4 They shall build up the ancient ruins;
   they shall raise up the former devastations;
they shall repair the ruined cities,
   the devastations of many generations.

____

____

____

____

____

Jesus states the essence of this abundant life: *I've come to give you freedom. I've come to heal your broken-heartedness. I've come to take your sadness and turn it to joy. I have come to take your oppression and bring it to happiness. I've come to bring the things that you've ruined and restore them.* His promises are given to all of us who will be living in and experiencing this troubled world—His promised super-abundant life.

What do these verses reveal about the nature of Christ and what He has come to do for us? What does this mean to how we are then to live? Why?

Read Colossians 1:12–23:

12 giving thanks[a] to the Father, who has qualified you[b] to share in the inheritance of the saints in light. 13 He has delivered us from the domain of darkness and transferred us to the kingdom of his beloved Son, 14 in whom we have redemption, the forgiveness of sins.

The Preeminence of Christ
15 He is the image of the invisible God, the firstborn of all creation. 16 For by[c] him all things were created, in heaven and on earth, visible and invisible, whether thrones or dominions or rulers or authorities—all things were created through him and for him. 17 And he is before all things, and in him all things hold together. 18 And he is the head of the body, the church. He is the beginning, the firstborn from the dead, that in everything he might be preeminent. 19 For in him all the fullness of God was pleased to dwell, 20 and through him to reconcile to himself all things, whether on earth or in heaven, making peace by the blood of his cross.

21 And you, who once were alienated and hostile in mind, doing evil deeds, 22 he has now reconciled in his body of flesh by his death, in order to present you holy and blameless and above reproach before him, 23 if indeed you continue in the faith, stable and steadfast, not shifting from the hope of the gospel that you heard, which has been proclaimed in all creation[d] under heaven, and of which I, Paul, became a minister.

____

____

____

____

____

Christ tells us that He has transferred us from darkness into His Kingdom. His Kingdom operates in a superior way to the world, which we know is controlled by the enemy: kill, steal, and destroy. Why is He superior to the material, natural world? Because He is the head of the body and all things were created by Him. All things were created by Him, for Him, with Him, and in Him. His spiritual power is superior to the world that we're involved with. He is preeminent and above all that. His Kingdom is above all that, but it doesn't negate that it's there with all its tribulation. Rather, given that the troubled world is where we live, His purpose is to reconcile each of us back to the fullness of the Kingdom. In Greek, this means to bring back to harmony the beautiful life that He had planned for you that you have lost. He is going to restore back to harmony the seven exceptional things that we covered in our course, _Abiding in the Vine_. These are the original elements of the spiritual life that are available to all who follow Him.

Will it be perfect like it was with Adam and Eve? No. How come? You're living in a wicked world that's under the control of the enemy. Who lives in this place? Sinful people, which includes us. So, is it even possible for it to be perfect? No, but His purpose is to restore back to you the life that He had planned for you. Because He is preeminent, He can deliver this. This super-abundant life is still available to us.

LESSON 1: GOD'S PURPOSE—LIVE IN ONENESS WITH HIM; OUR SPEAKING REFLECTS OUR HEART, WHICH IS IN A STRUGGLE BETWEEN THE FLESH AND THE SPIRIT.

In Genesis, God establishes the essence of His Covenant with all of us. What is the Covenant? What does this mean for our lives as believers? Why is this so important for us as we personally encounter life?

> **Read Genesis 12:1–3:**
>
> The Call of Abram
> **12** Now the LORD said[a] to Abram, "Go from your country[b] and your kindred and your father's house to the land that I will show you. 2 And I will make of you a great nation, and I will bless you and make your name great, so that you will be a blessing. 3 I will bless those who bless you, and him who dishonors you I will curse, and in you all the families of the earth shall be blessed."[c]

____

____

____

____

____

This promise from God is called the Covenant. The Covenant is really simple. He is going to bless you, give you super-abundant life, and restore you so that you, in turn, become a blessing, too. The life that He had planned and He is willing to give you is called a "flow through." It's not just to bless you and have you enjoy it by yourself—which is one of the primary benefits to us— but He is going to ask you to give it away. Give it away and be a representative of the heart that He has for fellow humans.

Think of the simplicity of what's being set up here. If you're going to give away blessing, how do you need to speak? In a way that is a blessing, but unfortunately, we tend not to speak this way. He wants you to receive the blessing, get excited about it, and then give it away. Let's explore this in greater detail.

This describes more specific details of the Covenant life. What is the condition to receive the benefits? What are all the benefits? Why is this so important to how we live?

Read Deuteronomy 28:1–14:

Blessings for Obedience

28 "And if you faithfully obey the voice of the LORD your God, being careful to do all his commandments that I command you today, the LORD your God will set you high above all the nations of the earth. [2] And all these blessings shall come upon you and overtake you, if you obey the voice of the LORD your God. [3] Blessed shall you be in the city, and blessed shall you be in the field. [4] Blessed shall be the fruit of your womb and the fruit of your ground and the fruit of your cattle, the increase of your herds and the young of your flock. [5] Blessed shall be your basket and your kneading bowl. [6] Blessed shall you be when you come in, and blessed shall you be when you go out.

[7] "The LORD will cause your enemies who rise against you to be defeated before you. They shall come out against you one way and flee before you seven ways. [8] The LORD will command the blessing on you in your barns and in all that you undertake. And he will bless you in the land that the LORD your God is giving you. [9] The LORD will establish you as a people holy to himself, as he has sworn to you, if you keep the commandments of the LORD your God and walk in his ways. [10] And all the peoples of the earth shall see that you are called by the name of the LORD, and they shall be afraid of you. [11] And the LORD will make you abound in prosperity, in the fruit of your womb and in the fruit of your livestock and in the fruit of your ground, within the land that the Lord swore to your fathers to give you. [12] The LORD will open to you his good treasury, the heavens, to give the rain to your land in its season and to bless all the work of your hands. And you shall lend to many nations, but you shall not borrow. [13] And the LORD will make you the head and not the tail, and you shall only go up and not down, if you obey the commandments of the LORD your God, which I command you today, being careful to do them, [14] and if you do not turn aside from any of the words that I command you today, to the right hand or to the left, to go after other gods to serve them.

In verses one and two, God says if you hear His voice and follow Him, what is going to happen? The blessings will literally overtake you, as is promised and is absolute. It's a guarantee. He is going to bless you for you then to become a blessing. However, if you turn around and chase the blessing, which means that you stopped hearing and following Him to pursue your own desires, what have you just done? You have essentially stopped the process of Him giving you the blessing. This is when you will have trouble, which leads to getting upset and speaking negatively. The key is to keep following Him. He is going to bless you to make you a blessing, but we still have a problem.

Adam and Eve were in the garden in perfect communion with God. God told them if they eat of a certain tree, they will surely die. Satan then comes along and tempts them to reject what God said and use their own free will to follow what Satan offers as a good idea. And they do. But, when they ate of the tree, they died. What died? Their spirit. Their spiritual connectivity to the perfect God and are now just flesh and soul. This is called a sinful nature.

Sinful nature is a self-centered nature that is driven by self and is now the nature of all their offspring, including us and our children and our grandchildren and their children, etc. We all have this sin nature and cannot overcome it. Why? Because of what happened with Adam and Eve. Because we all are born with this sinful nature, Jesus says that we all stand condemned because the requirement still needed is perfection. Jesus solved this problem, and took away that requirement. But now, because you're condemned, what must you do in order to not be condemned? Through belief, accept the gift of what He has fulfilled. This is how you become born again. This is also when the Spirit re-enters you so you can have a life with Him. If you're not born again, do you stand condemned? Yes. Do you spend eternity condemned? Yes. Because His work, His gift, has to be received in order to experience it.

LESSON 1: GOD'S PURPOSE—LIVE IN ONENESS WITH HIM; OUR SPEAKING REFLECTS OUR HEART, WHICH IS IN A STRUGGLE BETWEEN THE FLESH AND THE SPIRIT.

Christ has given us a promise for the super-abundant life. However, we have an enemy, the thief. What is his nature, and what has he come to do? Why is that problematic for us?

Read John 10:10:

10 The thief comes only to steal and kill and destroy. I came that they may have life and have it abundantly.

____

____

____

____

____

The nature of Satan is to kill, steal, and destroy. When? All the time. It's relentless. It characterizes the way he operates, and he has control over the world. We are not exempt from this and thus need to know how to address this.

As we deal with an enemy, principalities, and powers, how does the enemy work against us? How does this impact our receiving the super-abundant life that Christ has come to give us?

Read Ephesians 6:1–13:

Children and Parents
6 Children, obey your parents in the Lord, for this is right. 2 "Honor your father and mother" (this is the first commandment with a promise), 3 "that it may go well with you and that you may live long in the land." 4 Fathers, do not provoke your children to anger, but bring them up in the discipline and instruction of the Lord.

Bondservants and Masters

5 Bondservants,[a] obey your earthly masters[b] with fear and trembling, with a sincere heart, as you would Christ, 6 not by the way of eye-service, as people-pleasers, but as bondservants of Christ, doing the will of God from the heart, 7 rendering service with a good will as to the Lord and not to man, 8 knowing that whatever good anyone does, this he will receive back from the Lord, whether he is a bondservant or is free. 9 Masters, do the same to them, and stop your threatening, knowing that he who is both their Master[c] and yours is in heaven, and that there is no partiality with him.

The Whole Armor of God

10 Finally, be strong in the Lord and in the strength of his might. 11 Put on the whole armor of God, that you may be able to stand against the schemes of the devil. 12 For we do not wrestle against flesh and blood, but against the rulers, against the authorities, against the cosmic powers over this present darkness, against the spiritual forces of evil in the heavenly places. 13 Therefore take up the whole armor of God, that you may be able to withstand in the evil day, and having done all, to stand firm.

____

____

____

____

____

You've got an enemy, and scripture says you're dealing with his what? His *wiles*. In Greek, the word wiles means strategies and tactics—those things he is doing to thwart God's will. We need to understand that we are not dealing with flesh and blood that is already sinful and self-centered and naturally coming against you. We are instead dealing with what is behind that, which are principalities and powers. Satan has a whole host of those working against each of us. Their purpose is to draw you out of the Kingdom.

Is Satan God or does he have God's characteristics? No. Is he omnipresent? No. Is he omnipotent? No. Is he omniscient? No. We tend to think that we're in a battle of equals, but Satan is a created being and thus is limited, but he's got a lot of helpers, called the demonic.

The demonic, including Satan, used to be what? Angels. These angels chose to follow Satan, who is trying to overthrow God. Given that he has a lot of helpers, what are they doing? They're observing you. What are they looking for? Any reactive patterns we might have. For example, if something in particular happens, our reactive pattern goes to anger, or fear, or worry, or control, etc. The demonic are working you to do what? To speak negatively and go to resignation about those very things. The very pattern that took you into that place is revealed to you, and you speak negatively about the failure of the consequence of the pattern. You reinforce this issue through continual speaking of the struggle and the outcome, which is negative. The enemy is real. He observes our patterns and then hits our pattern to achieve the typical result—which we then speak to reinforce it.

The enemy is portrayed as a lion in these verses from Peter. What are these characteristics? How does that impact our ability to receive the super-abundant life?

Read 1 Peter 5:8:

[8] Be sober-minded; be watchful. Your adversary the devil prowls around like a roaring lion, seeking someone to devour.

____

____

____

____

____

A lion, all day long is on the prowl, on watch—for what? Prey, something to devour. What kind of prey? The weak ones—the ones that are struggling, or not quite capable, or falling behind. The lions can overcome all of them if they want to—which is why they are called the king of the jungle—but they generally just focus on the weak ones, which are easier to devour. The word *devour* means to destroy. Again, this is the nature of the enemy: kill, steal, and destroy. He is going to try to destroy you because you're weak. He knows this because he has observed this weakness. At what times are we weak? When we are not walking with God who is our strength.

What does Jesus say about what we will experience in this world? Why will all of us experience this? How does this impact how we live the super-abundant life? What are we to understand then about the conflicts and difficulties that we will encounter?

> **Jesus reinforces this in John 16:33:**
>
> [33] I have said these things to you, that in me you may have peace. In the world you will have tribulation. But take heart; I have overcome the world."

____

____

____

____

____

Jesus clearly says we who are living in the world are going to have trouble—stress, pressure, tribulation, difficult circumstances. If we remain in Christ, we will have shalom—the fullness of the super-abundant life—even in the middle of this troubled world. Does He exempt us from this? No. Does He put us in a bubble so we are fully protected from this? No. We are going to operate in the world, so you'll be in both places—the world and His Kingdom—at the same time. It doesn't exempt you from trouble. Why? Because the world is trouble.

What have we experienced this decade that we haven't experienced for the last severl years? Inflation. We're not used to this, and it is really taking its toll on us. Linda keeps telling me that the prices at the store are really going up. When I went to the store with her to see for myself, I couldn't believe it. Cans of pop that used to cost $2.50 for 12 are now $7.00. Almost three times higher. Certain cities are without drinking water or encounter frequent power outages. We're getting constantly impacted by the trouble of the world. God says: He doesn't exempt us from that, but He has answers for that.

When times are troubling, what do we have to say about it? My reaction to the price of soda pop was pretty much, *This is crazy. This is stupid. This is absurd. This makes me so mad.* God responded by asking, *How's it going? Why are you so upset about this? Does that surprise you?* The words coming out of your mouth influence your continual view and emotion and prevent you from living the grand, Covenant life that He has for you. Yes, in the world, you're going to have trouble, we're not exempt from that, but I wish you to see it and walk through it differently. One of the important aspects is to view this from a spiritual perspective.

What is the essence of the enemy's wiles and schemes for tempting us? Why do we fail with these temptations? What does this mean then to what is important for how we live?

> **Read James 1:12–18:**
>
> [12] Blessed is the man who remains steadfast under trial, for when he has stood the test he will receive the crown of life, which God has promised to those who love him. [13] Let no one say when he is tempted, "I am being tempted by God," for God cannot be tempted with evil, and he himself tempts no one. [14] But each person is tempted when he is lured and enticed by his own desire. [15] Then desire when it has conceived gives birth to sin, and sin when it is fully grown brings forth death.
>
> [16] Do not be deceived, my beloved brothers. [17] Every good gift and every perfect gift is from above, coming down from the Father of lights, with whom there is no variation or shadow due to change.[a] [18] Of his own will he brought us forth by the word of truth, that we should be a kind of firstfruits of his creatures.

____

____

____

____

____

Does God tempt you? No. He doesn't need to do that. There is plenty of trouble in the world, and He does not tempt you to fall farther into that trouble. He can bring trouble for a variety of purposes, but He does not tempt you to fail. Rather, temptation comes from the enemy. To what does he appeal to tempt you to? Yourself. Your own desire. He goes back to the appeal to Adam and Eve. *Don't you want to?* He will even take good ideas and twist them around. *Isn't this a good idea?* His intention is to get you to focus on your own decisions, what appeals to you in the flesh. He leads you to a point where you actually believe the direction he is taking you—even when underneath it all, you have a sense that it is not right and certainly not of God.

How do believers wind up in adultery? How do they justify it? They know it's not right. What do they say to themselves when this opportunity is before them? Maybe they like that the person is paying attention to them, or they believe that God will forgive them? Maybe they know a lot of Christians are also doing this, so it just doesn't seem so bad? Perhaps they have decided they would really enjoy this. The spouse isn't being supportive, and all they do is nag. They tell themselves they deserve to be happy.

The enemy appeals to your temptation, but then, your own speaking of what you believe and what you desire draws you out of the Kingdom of God. When you leave the Kingdom of God and act on it, God says that is when it turns to sin.

While there is certainly sin in the act that you commit, the real, greater sin is walking away from God through your self will. Now that you've exited out of the place where you can have the abundant life, you're going experience trouble. The enemy will constantly appeal to you to go to the flesh, to self, so that you remain outside the Kingdom. He cannot be with you in the Kingdom and overpower you there, but he will continue to appeal to your self will to pull you out so that you lose the protection and power of God. God tells us what happens as a result of that.

What does it mean to be in friendship with the world? What are the consequences of us being in friendship with the world? Why is this so important for how we then are going to live the super-abundant life?

Read James 4:1–4:

Warning Against Worldliness

4 What causes quarrels and what causes fights among you? Is it not this, that your passions[a] are at war within you?[b] 2 You desire and do not have, so you murder. You covet and cannot obtain, so you fight and quarrel. You do not have, because you do not ask. 3 You ask and do not receive, because you ask wrongly, to spend it on your passions. 4 You adulterous people![c] Do you not know that friendship with the world is enmity with God? Therefore whoever wishes to be a friend of the world makes himself an enemy of God.

Friendship with the world is enmity against God. God is not referring to enjoying the things of the world because He created them for us to enjoy. Rather, it's the system of the world that is under the control of the enemy, which is self-centeredness. When you live in a place of self-centeredness, or self-will, you automatically become an enemy of God.

When you become an enemy of God, who's working against you? The Lord—not because He wants to, but because you have gone to a position where you are working against God. You have chosen a place where there is going to be trouble, but God is inviting you to come back and follow Him.

We know that Satan is crafty, and one of the most effective tools in his toolbox is quarreling—arguing back and forth—your point against your opponent's. If you quarrel, it goes deeper and deeper and deeper. On what basis are you willing to go to battle? You believe you are right, and they are wrong, and you have decided that you need to persuade them that you are right. Depending on how much power or force you have, you continue to work it until they are either overcome or they cave and give up because they cannot win.

If you have power, what do you do? Run right over them, ignore them, go around them. It doesn't matter since you believe you can win. If the other person is also entrenched in their position and you go to battle openly, aggressively, and sometimes even legally, you are now fighting to see who's more powerful. Satan knows all about this. Jesus even spoke about this in Luke when He said a house divided will fall—it cannot stand.

The enemy is constantly working. Part of his method of destruction is to get a house divided. What can trigger this sort of reaction? Our words. If I attack Linda using harsh words, she will get defensive. This will result in her also speaking harshly to me. The enemy is trying to get us to do what? Oppose each other to the level of such division where we stop listening to each other. A house divided cannot stand. When a house is divided, Satan knows he's got you. He tempted you to self and then moved you to division—all through what you speak. If you do not process back with God, you stay divided and cannot stand.

What is a further consequence of being self-centered? Why?

> **Read Proverbs 18:1–2:**
>
> **18** Whoever isolates himself seeks his own desire;
>   he breaks out against all sound judgment.
> ² A fool takes no pleasure in understanding,
>   but only in expressing his opinion.

____

____

____

____

____

When all we care about is our own opinion and not respecting the process of working together toward God's solution, we are foolish. Self-centeredness is not caring about processing anything. The enemy is trying to get you to that point of foolishness; and it will be illustrated by the words you say. How do you play that out, and what's going on in your heart that is expressed by what you speak—especially when you are coming against somebody else? It shows that you are foolish—and you don't really care because you're getting your way. When you continue to reinforce it, you start getting defensive because you are convinced you are right and others simply aren't. You, then, go into attack mode instead of listening and processing with a heart to seek unity and God's answers. You aren't even listening to what others are saying, you are just formulating your next argument. You are not trying to understand, but rather win.

Recently there was noticeable tension in the church regarding Covid and the Covid vaccine. There was very little discussion or listening. People took their stance, believed they were right, and tried to persuade everyone else of their position. If others did not agree, the tension rose as both sides tried to silence those who opposed them. This caused great division and conflict in the church and even in families—where groups and individuals would no longer attend functions together or even speak to each other.

Division, not listening to others, trying to force your agenda—these are just a few of the reasons we need to learn God's principles for life.

Principles of Learning How to Speak in the Life of God:

As we learn how to receive, live, and speak the life of God, what is important for us to understand about the nature and purpose of God? What then does this mean for how we approach everyday life with troubles and an enemy that is attempting to thwart our super-abundant life? Why?

Read Psalm 111:1–10:

Great Are the LORD'S Works
111 [a] Praise the LORD!
I will give thanks to the LORD with my whole heart,
    in the company of the upright, in the congregation.
² Great are the works of the LORD,
    studied by all who delight in them.

> [3] Full of splendor and majesty is his work,
>   and his righteousness endures forever.
> [4] He has caused his wondrous works to be remembered;
>   the LORD is gracious and merciful.
> [5] He provides food for those who fear him;
>   he remembers his covenant forever.
> [6] He has shown his people the power of his works,
>   in giving them the inheritance of the nations.
> [7] The works of his hands are faithful and just;
>   all his precepts are trustworthy;
> [8] they are established forever and ever,
>   to be performed with faithfulness and uprightness.
> [9] He sent redemption to his people;
>   he has commanded his covenant forever.
>   Holy and awesome is his name!
> [10] The fear of the LORD is the beginning of wisdom;
>   all those who practice it have a good understanding.
>   His praise endures forever!

____

____

____

____

____

The first of God's principles for life is: God is for us. He's ever mindful of the Covenant—He will bless you to make you a blessing. This is His foundation for all of life, for all of us who are believers, for all of our life—all the time. He is ever mindful of the Covenant—in whatever you are facing—all that you wrote down at the beginning of this lesson—no matter how sticky, complicated, tough to maneuver, or difficult to resolve. Right now, at this very moment, God is saying, "I have this covered, I am going to resolve this for you, I am going to bless you to make you a blessing. Yes, I know you have trouble. I know it's a sticky thing. I know this is not working out for you—but I will always deliver the Covenant." And then He says, "I will command the Covenant. I'm thinking about it. I'm getting you ready to receive it."

If He commands the Covenant, what does that mean? It's going to happen. It is deeply profound and deeply true—all the time. He is going to deliver the Covenant. The Covenant is an agreement, but in order for Him to deliver the Covenant, we have to be with Him. He cannot deliver it when we are not with Him. We have already learned that we can walk away from Him and He will not force us to stay or to return. It is a choice we have to make. When we do walk away, the good news is that He has a simple remedy: repent and come back. When we return, He welcomes us back and delivers the Covenant.

What is necessary for God to command blessing into our lives? What does this mean for us? Why?

Read Psalm 133:

When Brothers Dwell in Unity
A Song of Ascents. Of David.
133 Behold, how good and pleasant it is
    when brothers dwell in unity![a]
2 It is like the precious oil on the head,
    running down on the beard,
on the beard of Aaron,
    running down on the collar of his robes!
3 It is like the dew of Hermon,
    which falls on the mountains of Zion!
For there the Lord has commanded the blessing,
    life forevermore.

____

____

____

____

____

Another key principle is that God will command blessing when we dwell in unity. Think how simple and beautiful this is: God is ever mindful of the Covenant and thus always wants to command Covenant to us—He just needs us to join Him. We can join Him through unity. Unity isn't just between two or more negotiating a compromise—it's coming and seeking His will, understanding His will, and confirming His will. It is unity together with Him. When we discover this, we discover His will and, thus, join Him in delivering the Covenant to us.

He has given us the privilege of processing together with a spouse, with a friend, with our inner circle—to reach confirmation of His will together. It is there He delivers the Covenant and commands blessing. We have learned that this means it will happen in real life. It's not a natural, logical process, but a spiritual process with Him that has a big implication for how we speak to each other. No longer will we be persuading or debating or complaining. We understand we all have issues and problems and differing opinions. That's okay. But if we go together to see what God has to say, that is a far different conversation. We are to assist each other in going to truth and discovering God's will where we will receive His promised Covenant.

Read the following three verses. As we are learning the principles of how we are to live and how we are to speak, what is important to understand about what our speaking is really about? Why is this so important for us to know?

Read Proverbs 23:7:

[7] for he is like one who is inwardly calculating.[a]
  "Eat and drink!" he says to you,
  but his heart is not with you.

____

____

____

____

____

What you speak and what you think is really a reflection of what? Your heart. What's the definition of the heart? Your soul, which is the essence of who you are, the seat of your will, intellect, personality, emotion. What's going on in your soul is a reflection of your true self and thus what you speak reflects your true self—so speaking is a heart issue.

Read Matthew 12:33–37:

A Tree Is Known by Its Fruit

33 "Either make the tree good and its fruit good, or make the tree bad and its fruit bad, for the tree is known by its fruit. 34 You brood of vipers! How can you speak good, when you are evil? For out of the abundance of the heart the mouth speaks. 35 The good person out of his good treasure brings forth good, and the evil person out of his evil treasure brings forth evil. 36 I tell you, on the day of judgment people will give account for every careless word they speak, 37 for by your words you will be justified, and by your words you will be condemned."

Jesus says that when you look at a tree, you can observe something. What do you observe? Its fruit. Does it have any fruit or not? Is it alive or dead? It's really easy to see that. He says, "Out of the heart is going to come your fruit." One of the key elements of fruit is what you say. This is significant because what you say is a reflection your heart. If you have goodness, then you'll speak goodness. If you have evil, then you'll speak evil. The word *evil* used in these verses doesn't mean dark or awful, it means things that annoy, frustrate, and irritate you. So, if that's what you're speaking, it reflects what is going on inside your heart—you're concerned, you're worried, you're fearful, you're anxious. The truth and the things of God are not being reflected because you have not allowed His nature and His power into your heart. So instead of living in peace and joy, believers are living in heaviness and burden—and what they are speaking reflects that.

Read Luke 6:43–45:

A Tree and Its Fruit

43 "For no good tree bears bad fruit, nor again does a bad tree bear good fruit, 44 for each tree is known by its own fruit. For figs are not gathered from thornbushes, nor are grapes picked from a bramble bush. 45 The good person out of the good treasure of his heart produces good, and the evil person out of his evil treasure produces evil, for out of the abundance of the heart his mouth speaks.

Again, Jesus makes a very simple statement. A good tree produces what? Good fruit. A tree that is not good produces what? Bad fruit. This will be easy to decipher which is which. Jesus goes a little bit deeper when He says it's not just your experience, but also how you view the experience—which is reflected in what you say about the experience.

When something really good happens, some people say the other shoe is about to drop, this won't last, or bad things are coming. Even though they just experienced something wonderful, the expectation is that it isn't going to last, so they should prepare for the bad thing that is coming next. The fruit is a reflection of your heart beliefs and thus how you operate in life.

How do these verses describe the basis of how we speak? What does that mean? Why is this so important then to how we learn to speak the life of God?

Read 2 Corinthians 4:11–15:

[11] For we who live are always being given over to death for Jesus' sake, so that the life of Jesus also may be manifested in our mortal flesh. [12] So death is at work in us, but life in you.

[13] Since we have the same spirit of faith according to what has been written, "I believed, and so I spoke," we also believe, and so we also speak, [14] knowing that he who raised the Lord Jesus will raise us also with Jesus and bring us with you into his presence. [15] For it is all for your sake, so that as grace extends to more and more people it may increase thanksgiving, to the glory of God.

____

____

____

____

____

God gives us this interesting truth: You speak what you believe, so anyone can understand what you believe by just listening to you talk. If you are having difficulty and you are speaking negatively, complaining, grumbling, or having fear, then you expect the difficulty to be more problematic and end up going to fear, worry, and anxiety. Does it do any good for someone to tell you to stop talking that way? No. However, since they know what you believe based upon your words, they can invite you to learn what God has to say given that He can bring resolution for every issue you have. They can help you learn that God will change your belief to the truth. There's a choice to make—are you willing to go, or would you rather wallow in your misery? While we all have fundamental problems with our beliefs, choose to allow God to change yours.

With a heart to grow in our belief (faith), what is our fundamental problem? How does this impact our receiving the super-abundant life? Why?

Read Romans 7:13–24:

[13] Did that which is good, then, bring death to me? By no means! It was sin, producing death in me through what is good, in order that sin might be shown to be sin, and through the commandment might become sinful beyond measure. [14] For we know that the law is spiritual, but I am of the flesh, sold under sin. [15] For I do not understand my own actions. For I do not do what I want, but I do the very thing I hate. [16] Now if I do what I do not want, I agree with the law, that it is good. [17] So now it is no longer I who do it, but sin that dwells within me. [18] For I know that nothing good dwells in me, that is, in my flesh. For I have the desire to do what is right, but not the ability to carry it out. [19] For I do not do the good I want, but the evil I do not want is what I keep on doing. [20] Now if I do what I do not want, it is no longer I who do it, but sin that dwells within me.

[21] So I find it to be a law that when I want to do right, evil lies close at hand. [22] For I delight in the law of God, in my inner being, [23] but I see in my members another law waging war against the law of my mind and making me captive to the law of sin that dwells in my members. [24] Wretched man that I am! Who will deliver me from this body of death?

____

____

____

____

____

Paul says, "Of all believers, I am one with the greatest heart to follow God." Following God was not the problem. "But, I find I have a fundamental problem because of my nature. The things that I shouldn't do, I do; and the things that I'm supposed to do, I don't." It's not because he didn't have a heart to do it, and it wasn't because of his personal deficiency. So, then, what was the problem? The flesh—sin nature. Had Paul grown in Christ? Yes. Did he know a lot of truth? Yes. Why does he still have the problem? Because of the sin nature. Unfortunately, this nature doesn't get any better, and it won't permanently leave. Do you grow in Christ? Yes. Do you get sanctified? Yes, but only if you stay with Him and do not live in the flesh. We all have a problem—the self, which is our default.

In verse 24, Paul writes, "Oh wretched man am I! Who can save me from this awful situation?" If the answer was nothing and no one, what would he have done? Stopped writing and accepted that he was going to live with difficulty and burden. Fortunately, he had an answer. The answer is a life of Christ.

When will you have problems? All the time—and it'll be reflected by what you say. How are you speaking about this? How are you acting? How are you functioning? We are not to stay with this problem, but learn to receive and experience the life of Christ, which is the solution to this problem.

If we continue to live with the problem that Paul describes in Romans 7, what are the consequences? What do these mean then to our ability to receive the super-abundant life? Why?

Read Romans 8:5–8:

5 For those who live according to the flesh set their minds on the things of the flesh, but those who live according to the Spirit set their minds on the things of the Spirit. 6 For to set the mind on the flesh is death, but to set the mind on the Spirit is life and peace. 7 For the mind that is set on the flesh is hostile to God, for it does not submit to God's law; indeed, it cannot. 8 Those who are in the flesh cannot please God.

Remember, the flesh is what Paul just described—it's the self that is your default. So, either you're going to walk in the Spirit, which can overcome this problem, or remain in the flesh—by default. If you remain in the flesh, there are consequences:

1. You put to death the work of the Spirit and operate as if it's not there anymore. You essentially go back to what Adam and Eve did when they followed their own self will and died. In doing this, you also put to death the Spirit.

2. You are at enmity against God. How is that going to work out for you? Now, He's working against you. You are already in the world where the enemy has power over you and is bringing about trouble for you. Jesus said that even when you're walking in the Spirit, you're going to have trouble. Well, guess what? When you're not walking in the Spirit, you compound the trouble. Not only that, but you're contributing to it. So, what's the purpose of God causing even more trouble? He's trying to get your attention so He can invite you to come back to His life and the solution to the problem.

3. You can't please Him. This is a spiritual problem that causes us to speak negatively. Are you in the flesh? Because, if you're in the flesh, you're spiritually at a place where you can't go back to the positive. Circumstances are going to get more oppressive, more difficult, heavier, and you will not be able to find resolution, but then Jesus tells us a great story about this.

What is really at the center of our problem of the flesh? What is important to understand about this and why?

Read Matthew 16:13–23:

Peter Confesses Jesus as the Christ

13 Now when Jesus came into the district of Caesarea Philippi, he asked his disciples, "Who do people say that the Son of Man is?" 14 And they said, "Some say John the Baptist, others say Elijah, and others Jeremiah or one of the prophets." 15 He said to them, "But who do you say that I am?" 16 Simon Peter replied, "You are the Christ, the Son of the living God." 17 And Jesus answered him, "Blessed are you, Simon Bar-Jonah! For flesh and blood has not revealed this to you, but my Father who is in heaven. 18 And I tell you, you are Peter,

and on this rock[a] I will build my church, and the gates of hell[b] shall not prevail against it. [19] I will give you the keys of the kingdom of heaven, and whatever you bind on earth shall be bound in heaven, and whatever you loose on earth shall be loosed[c] in heaven." [20] Then he strictly charged the disciples to tell no one that he was the Christ.

Jesus Foretells His Death and Resurrection

[21] From that time Jesus began to show his disciples that he must go to Jerusalem and suffer many things from the elders and chief priests and scribes, and be killed, and on the third day be raised. [22] And Peter took him aside and began to rebuke him, saying, "Far be it from you, Lord![d] This shall never happen to you." [23] But he turned and said to Peter, "Get behind me, Satan! You are a hindrance[e] to me. For you are not setting your mind on the things of God, but on the things of man."

____

____

____

____

____

As the disciples were walking together with Jesus, He says, "Who do people say I am?" They responded saying, John the Baptist. Elijah. Jeremiah. Jesus then asked them, "Who do you say I am?" Peter says, "You are the Christ, the Son of the living God. You're the Messiah." This pleased Jesus, and He explained that Peter couldn't understand this in his own thinking, but instead he received it through God's revelation. When Peter spoke of who Jesus was, he demonstrated his ability to receive and to discern God's will.

Christ said He was going to build His church upon this process: hearing Him speak, believing what He says, and then taking His authority and exercising His power—binding off the power of Satan and loosing the power of heaven into every situation so that He can deliver to you the Covenant. It is then He will say, "Well done."

Jesus goes on to tell His disciples that He is going to Jerusalem, and He is going to be beaten, and He will suffer. He tells them He is going to die—but He will be resurrected. Upon hearing this, what does Peter say? "I will never let that happen to you." And then he rebukes Jesus.

When you rebuke someone, what are you doing? Telling them that what they are saying is wrong. To Jesus, it was more than Peter saying he would never let that happen. He was telling Jesus He was wrong. Jesus responds saying, "Get behind Me, Satan." In a span of 20 minutes, Peter went from the most holy person to Satan. Why? Because he did not have the things of God in mind, but the things of men. He was acting out of self without even considering seeking God and what He has to say about it.

What is the mistake that Peter made? He didn't seek or ask God. He decided on his own—in the flesh—what he was going to do. What he said, reflected his heart and what he believed. But after hearing his words, Jesus said, "Either you have the things of God in your heart or the things of man," and He will know by what you say. The words Peter spoke showed that his heart was filled with the things of man.

God wants us to understand that He wants to deliver the Covenant to all of us, all the time. He wants to bless us to be made a blessing. He wants us to have the things of God in our heart so that the words we use reflect Him.

We are to understand that God's desire is to give us the super-abundant life. So, when we have trouble, which is all the time, God wants us to stand on our belief of the Covenant—that He will resolve this and make all things good. The enemy is trying to pull you away from His ability to give you this resolution, this super-abundant life. Because of this, we are to assist each other in seeking and receiving God and what He speaks. We need to help each other discover this through unity—with your spouse, friend, inner circle. We need to help each other seek God and experience the Covenant.

We speak what is in our heart—this is what we believe. Unfortunately, our default is the sin nature of the self where we seek the things of men and not God. We fail to seek Him and ask Him what He has to say about our troubles. As we move into Lessons 2 and 3, we will learn how to overcome this issue of the flesh and experience God. Once we overcome this, our new heart and our new beliefs will be reflected.

LESSON 2: ABIDING, SPENDING TIME WITH HIM TO RECEIVE HIS HEART THAT BECOMES OUR HEART; WHAT NOT TO SPEAK AND WHAT WE ARE TO SPEAK.

As we continue this course: *We Are What We Speak*, we've learned that our heart is reflected by what we say—our words communicate what we believe. In order for us to speak the way that God wants us to speak, what's inside of us—our beliefs—need to change.

We have learned that God's goal is to give us a super-abundant life, give us the Covenant. He is ever mindful of the Covenant. We know we have an enemy, and that enemy is trying to draw us away from the life of God to affect what we believe. This is what happened with Adam and Eve. They had not received and believed what God had to say, so they decided in the flesh to disobey and then the spiritual life they enjoyed died. What we say matters, and since our words reflect our heart and our beliefs, we need to learn how to follow God and receive His heart so that what we speak reflects His nature and not the self. In this lesson, we will learn just that—how to follow God and to have Him change our heart. This change also will become clear to others as they hear the words we speak.

How does Micaiah respond to the king who asks him to speak certain things? What does that mean for us? Why are we to follow this in our lives?

> **"What we say matters, and since our words reflect our heart and our beliefs, we need to learn how to follow God and receive His heart so that what we speak reflects His nature and not the self."**

Read 1 Kings 22:13–14:

Micaiah Prophesies Against Ahab

13 And the messenger who went to summon Micaiah said to him, "Behold, the words of the prophets with one accord are favorable to the king. Let your word be like the word of one of them, and speak favorably." 14 But Micaiah said, "As the Lord lives, what the Lord says to me, that I will speak."

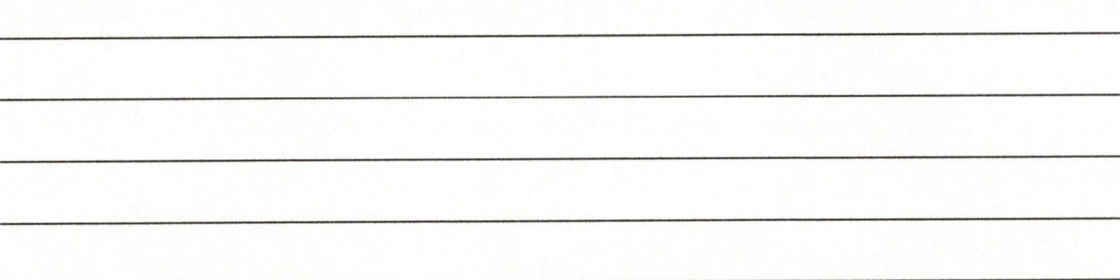

____

____

____

____

____

Here, the messenger from the king tells Micaiah that the prophets are only telling the king things that he would find favorable or encouraging, and the king wants Micaiah to do the same. How does Micaiah respond? He tells the messenger that he will only say what God tells him to say. He knows what the others are saying and knows that what they are proclaiming—their words— are not of God. Micaiah would only speak what God revealed to him. If we are to do the same and speak only what God reveals to us, we need to pay attention to what He is saying, consistently listening as we stay in intimate relationship with Him, and continue to process with Him until we fully understand with clarity what He has to say to us. Only then can we also share His message with others. We need to have a heart that always seeks the Father, asking Him what He wants us to say to others.

What does God say to Jeremiah regarding how he is to speak the things of God? What does that mean then for how we live the super-abundant life God is giving us? Why?

> **Read Jeremiah 1:4–10:**
>
> The Call of Jeremiah
> [4] Now the word of the LORD came to me, saying,
> [5] "Before I formed you in the womb I knew you,
> and before you were born I consecrated you;
> I appointed you a prophet to the nations."
>
> [6] Then I said, "Ah, LORD GOD! Behold, I do not know how to speak, for I am only a youth." [7] But the LORD said to me,

> "Do not say, 'I am only a youth';
> for to all to whom I send you, you shall go,
> and whatever I command you, you shall speak.
> 8 Do not be afraid of them,
> for I am with you to deliver you,
> declares the LORD."
>
> 9 Then the LORD put out his hand and touched my mouth. And the LORD said to me,
>
> "Behold, I have put my words in your mouth.
> 10 See, I have set you this day over nations and over kingdoms,
> to pluck up and to break down,
> to destroy and to overthrow,
> to build and to plant."

____

____

____

____

____

God tells Jeremiah that He is going to send him out to deliver His messages—to speak for Him. How does Jeremiah respond? He gives God a list of reasons why he is not fit for the job. He's too young, he doesn't know how to speak well, he's just not good enough. But God knew it wasn't about Jeremiah's skill or ability or experience—or lack thereof—it was about God. The only thing Jeremiah needed to do was receive and follow what God spoke and speak the words that God gave him.

As you come to understand this, you will begin to see that most of your energy is going to be spent listening, processing, and understanding what God is saying. Once the message is clearly understood, you can go speak it. But until you believe it, receive it, and understand it, it would be better not to say a whole lot.

The key to the process is to have a heart to hear what the Father has to say, to stay with Him and dialogue with Him until He gives clarity and understanding, and then, with this clarity, speak it—to yourself, to those around you, and then to the specific situation that God indicates. If you process things this way, God says His word will be super powerful and purposeful.

What can God do with His words that He asks us to speak? He can make things happen. He can cast off the work of the enemy. He can bring His power to the situation. When we speak His words, we are the vessel God is using to express Himself. He does that through the Holy Spirit that is within us. We are the way He fulfills His purpose and His will here on Earth.

Regardless of our circumstances, what are we to believe about how we approach this? What does God promise us, and how does this change how we speak? Why?

> **Read Matthew 10:19–20:**
>
> [19] When they deliver you over, do not be anxious how you are to speak or what you are to say, for what you are to say will be given to you in that hour. [20] For it is not you who speak, but the Spirit of your Father speaking through you.

____

____

____

____

____

This is a pure statement. Don't worry about the situation into which you're going to speak. Why? Because this is God's call, and He will show you and tell you how to speak. He will remind you of the truth you already have processed. He will bring clarity and understanding. All of this implies that you're walking in the Spirit, and you are sensitive to the voice of God. The purity is that you do not have to figure this out. You don't have to try to figure out how to execute God's will, or come up with alternative plans, or prepare for crossing bridges that you never get to. We are all to simply let God speak, let Him give us truth and encouragement, and let Him show us what we are then to speak—His life and His will. The more you practice it, the easier it becomes.

LESSON 2: ABIDING, SPENDING TIME WITH HIM TO RECEIVE HIS HEART THAT BECOMES OUR HEART; WHAT NOT TO SPEAK AND WHAT WE ARE TO SPEAK.

How did Christ relate to the Father? What did that mean for Christ's carrying out the life of God? Why is this the way we are also to relate to the Father? Why?

Read John 8:26–30:

26 I have much to say about you and much to judge, but he who sent me is true, and I declare to the world what I have heard from him." 27 They did not understand that he had been speaking to them about the Father. 28 So Jesus said to them, "When you have lifted up the Son of Man, then you will know that I am he, and that I do nothing on my own authority, but speak just as the Father taught me. 29 And he who sent me is with me. He has not left me alone, for I always do the things that are pleasing to him." 30 As he was saying these things, many believed in him.

____

____

____

____

____

Jesus said He will only speak what the Father (through the Spirit) has spoken. So, what He hears from the Father, He will speak out. The importance here is His focus. It doesn't mean that He cannot talk without fully checking in, but rather what the Father speaks, He receives and then speaks. If He has something that comes up, He will check in, but He is always available to be checked and interrupted with something that the Father wishes to say. We are to be in that same place regarding what we speak. We are to operate in the same way because we are the physical representative of the invisible God, and we have Him through the Holy Spirit living within us. His words have life and power.

How does Christ describe the words that He speaks to us? What is the difference between these words and the flesh? What is then important for us to understand about receiving Christ's words for us?

> **Read John 6:63:**
>
> [63] It is the Spirit who gives life; the flesh is no help at all. The words that I have spoken to you are spirit and life.

____

____

____

____

____

His words are both logos (the Bible, the Word) and rhema (what He speaks personally to us). If you try to interpret this and put your spin on it, this counts for what? Nothing. We thus can gather no meaning from our own logic and our own perspective. But His words that you're hearing and receiving, and then speaking are what? Spirit and life.

It's more than just having a positive attitude or looking at His Word as principle, law, rules to follow, or something that is nice and pleasant. It's really about the power of what He is saying to us. When you understand this, you move to being His representative with authority—where you can speak power and truth into situations, into scenarios, into yourself. These are not just good ideas, but the very power to deliver what these words speak.

LESSON 2: ABIDING, SPENDING TIME WITH HIM TO RECEIVE HIS HEART THAT BECOMES OUR HEART; WHAT NOT TO SPEAK AND WHAT WE ARE TO SPEAK.

Instead of thinking of the spiritual life as a periodic Bible study, what is important for us to understand regarding our everyday relationship with God? What does this mean to us and why?

How often are we called to receive and understand His Word to us? Every day, all the time. We are always to be in the process of hearing what He has to say. God will speak about our personal issues and circumstances—what's going on in our lives right now. This is why we are to have a heart to hear what He is speaking and revealing to us. When we process His words through to understanding and clarity, we will know what steps we are to take, we will know if we are to go farther or deeper into a situation, and we will know what God is asking us to speak into other situations.

God says He is going to give us words. What is the essence of these words, and what does that mean? How then are we to approach life with trouble and difficulty? Why?

Read Jeremiah 11:1–6:

The Broken Covenant

11 The word that came to Jeremiah from the LORD: [2] "Hear the words of this covenant, and speak to the men of Judah and the inhabitants of Jerusalem. [3] You shall say to them, Thus says the LORD, the God of Israel: Cursed be the man who does not hear the words of this covenant [4] that I commanded your fathers when I brought them out of the land of Egypt, from the iron furnace, saying, Listen to my voice, and do all that I command you. So shall you be my people, and I will be your God, [5] that I may confirm the oath that I swore to your fathers, to give them a land flowing with milk and honey, as at this day." Then I answered, "So be it, LORD."

[6] And the LORD said to me, "Proclaim all these words in the cities of Judah and in the streets of Jerusalem: Hear the words of this covenant and do them.

God says that the words He is going to give you are the words of the Covenant. This is very interesting. He is establishing the Covenant (we will be blessed to be made a blessing) as the basis of how we are to live and thus receive what He has to say in each situation of our lives. God reminds us that He is ever mindful of the Covenant and that He will command the Covenant. This means that what He speaks will guide us and lead us into experiencing the Covenant. Everything in our lives will then be viewed from that perspective. The words of the Covenant are your starting point.

Since we are to speak the words of the Covenant, what exactly is the Covenant? What does this mean then for how we approach all our circumstances of life, including those that are difficult and cause us trouble? Why?

Read Genesis 12:1–3:

The Call of Abram

12 Now the LORD said[a] to Abram, "Go from your country[b] and your kindred and your father's house to the land that I will show you. 2 And I will make of you a great nation, and I will bless you and make your name great, so that you will be a blessing. 3 I will bless those who bless you, and him who dishonors you I will curse, and in you all the families of the earth shall be blessed."[c]

____

____

____

____

As we begin to understand how to walk through life and speak His words, we are to always start with a firm belief in the words of the Covenant. We know that He will speak the Covenant into every circumstance—that is His answer to our issue, to our difficult circumstances. He knows things are tough and that we experience a lot of trouble. He understands that, but He also knows that He is going to deliver the Covenant. He is going to bless each of us so that we, in turn, can also be a blessing. Believing that God will deliver the Covenant to us, translates into processing and receiving His words and ultimately speaking them. We can be assured of this because, through the Holy Spirit, He lives within us.

Since we are to receive and speak the Covenant, what is the good news regarding how we are able to fulfill this every day? What does that mean then for how we live this way? Why?

Read Jeremiah 31:31–34:

The New Covenant

[31] "Behold, the days are coming, declares the LORD, when I will make a new covenant with the house of Israel and the house of Judah, [32] not like the covenant that I made with their fathers on the day when I took them by the hand to bring them out of the land of Egypt, my covenant that they broke, though I was their husband, declares the LORD. [33] For this is the covenant that I will make with the house of Israel after those days, declares the LORD: I will put my law within them, and I will write it on their hearts. And I will be their God, and they shall be my people. [34] And no longer shall each one teach his neighbor and each his brother, saying, 'Know the LORD,' for they shall all know me, from the least of them to the greatest, declares the LORD. For I will forgive their iniquity, and I will remember their sin no more."

____

____

____

____

____

God says that He has not only given us the Covenant but will also work our side of the agreement by placing Himself within each of us. We will be able to hear His voice and follow what He has to say—and then we will be able to speak it out. It is not a matter of doing our best to get everything right, rather, it is simply being with God and experiencing His life that is within us.

God promises to speak the words of the Covenant. He will give it to us, and we will be able to receive it. Why? Because when we walk with Him, we have one heart with His and are able to hear what He has to say to us. This is the beauty of the Holy Spirit. When you become a believer, you become born again. What enters you? God, the Father; God, the Son; and God, the Holy Spirit. He said: We make Our home with you. So, God, the Father, is speaking, and the Holy Spirit is listening and translating God's words to you because He's in there, living inside you. That is His job and it shows why it's so important to learn what it means to hear His voice. It is a spiritual activity. It's not a mechanical one or an intellectual one, and it's not theology. It's a beautiful life of God who is expressing the truth into your situations.

I was pondering this once about the Holy Spirit, and God had a dialogue with me:

God: "Rich, where am I?"

Rich: "You are in me."

God: "When people are questioning that, it's all about logic and theology. Ask them this question: What do you think I'm doing in there?"

Rich: "Most people actually think the answer is nothing. You're just waiting for us to die and take us to heaven."

God: "Yes, the reason is because there's no interaction with Me. There's no response to what I'm saying or doing. Everyone is trying to figure everything out by themselves."

Rich: "Which means they are in the flesh and have put to death the Spirit."

God: "My heart is to reveal to you My will and tell you what to speak, how to move forward, how to be obedient so that you are in the place for Me to deliver to you the Covenant. This includes when you are struggling, in trouble, or experiencing ruin and loss."

Because of the trouble of the world, we often experience ruin and loss. What does God promise about this? What are the details of what we can expect? What is our role in the process? Why?

Read Zechariah 8:11–13; 16–17:

[11] But now I will not deal with the remnant of this people as in the former days, declares the Lord of hosts. [12] For there shall be a sowing of peace. The vine shall give its fruit, and the ground shall give its produce, and the heavens shall give their dew. And I will cause the remnant of this people to possess all these things. [13] And as you have been a byword of cursing among the nations, O house of Judah and house of Israel, so will I save you, and you shall be a blessing. Fear not, but let your hands be strong."

[16] These are the things that you shall do: Speak the truth to one another; render in your gates judgments that are true and make for peace; [17] do not devise evil in your hearts against one another, and love no false oath, for all these things I hate, declares the LORD."

____

____

____

____

____

God says He is going to restore you. His words are going to become prosperous in your life. You're going to have circumstances change. He is going to bless you to make you a blessing. He is going to have you experience the life of the Holy Spirit. He is going to deliver fruit when you abide in Him. He is ready to deliver all this to you, and He's operating in you to make you a blessing. If you are in a place where you are receiving all of this, you're also going to be in a place where you will give it away—where you will speak to others and invite them to this same abiding relationship, which is the very heart of God.

The Holy Spirit is showing you truth in order for you to speak truth. He further said for us to make judgment in your gate. Remember, at the gate is where people met with the leaders of the city to process decisions together until they discovered God's will. So, He wants us to stay with it until we discover His will—which is the Covenant.

God also says: Don't speak evil to each other. What does that mean? Remember, evil doesn't mean dark or awful, rather, it means things not of God that annoy, frustrate, irritate, and cause trouble. "Don't speak evil to each other" means not to reinforce it in your heart and mind by speaking about how awful it is or how terrible or how it will never work. By speaking evil, you reinforce that belief, which then leads you to work harder to resolve the issue on your own or go to resignation. God says: Why don't you go with Me and speak life? Why don't you ask Me to tell you what I have to say? In seeking Him, He will provide the Covenant—resolution.

In addition, don't make false vows. Do not promise to be there for someone without following through on that promise. God says that in order to receive His promised resolution, we are to speak the truth, process until we receive His will, keep speaking life—not evil, and have integrity—fully believing and knowing that He will restore each and every one of us.

When we find ourselves in difficult circumstances, what are we to believe and understand? What does that mean then for how we approach these troubling things? Why?

> **Read Matthew 10:19–20:**
>
> [19] When they deliver you over, do not be anxious how you are to speak or what you are to say, for what you are to say will be given to you in that hour. [20] For it is not you who speak, but the Spirit of your Father speaking through you.

____

____

____

____

____

God says that we will find ourselves in situations that are difficult, oppressive, and seemingly unresolvable. This is not a matter of *if* but *when*. However, we are not to worry about how to process through this, in particular we are not to worry about how to respond and speak. Why? Because the Holy Spirit is assigned to guide you and reveal to you what to speak—that is His role. Our role is to seek it, trust it, and follow it—with a confidence that He will always lead us to the Covenant. He knows of every problem we have, but He will guide us, and we will know how to respond to move down His path for each of us individually.

Why is not having the demonic speak so significant to us? How does God use this for our benefit? Why?

Read Mark 1:32–34:

32 That evening at sundown they brought to him all who were sick or oppressed by demons. 33 And the whole city was gathered together at the door. 34 And he healed many who were sick with various diseases, and cast out many demons. And he would not permit the demons to speak, because they knew him.

There was sickness, and there was the demonic. What did Jesus do? Healed them all and cast out all the demonic. While Jesus was healing the sick and casting out demons, He did not allow the demonic to speak. There is a very profound reason for this. If you're drifting into evil, into the flesh, He's going to check you so you are aware that you are heading in the wrong direction and the words you are about to speak are not of Him. When words spoken are not of Him, you are operating in the flesh.

In business, there have been situations where I have come close to overreacting and speaking something that was clearly not of God. In each of these times, the Spirit checked me and said, "Rich, if I were you, I wouldn't say what you are about to say—that is not of Me. It is of the flesh—evil, and I am asking you not to speak it." He has the power to have you understand that you are headed toward goodness or walking the opposite direction, so pay attention. Let's look at how we receive this. How do we hear His voice?

What is important for us to learn as we are desiring to speak what God wants us to speak? What does that mean to us and why?

Read Psalm 145:17–21:

17 The LORD is righteous in all his ways
and kind in all his works.
18 The LORD is near to all who call on him,
to all who call on him in truth.
19 He fulfills the desire of those who fear him;
he also hears their cry and saves them.
20 The LORD preserves all who love him,
but all the wicked he will destroy.
21 My mouth will speak the praise of the LORD,
and let all flesh bless his holy name forever and ever.

____

____

____

____

Our heart is really for what? To seek Him. Before you speak, before you exercise the flesh, seek to hear from the Spirit. It starts with the fear of the Lord. What is the fear of the Lord? Scripture has revelation for this.

LESSON 2: ABIDING, SPENDING TIME WITH HIM TO RECEIVE HIS HEART THAT BECOMES OUR HEART; WHAT NOT TO SPEAK AND WHAT WE ARE TO SPEAK.

Reading through these verses, what does it mean to fear the Lord? How does this impact how we approach the things of our lives? Why is this so important to how we walk through this?

Read Psalm 19:7–11:

7 The law of the LORD is perfect,[a]
   reviving the soul;
the testimony of the LORD is sure,
   making wise the simple;
8 the precepts of the LORD are right,
   rejoicing the heart;
the commandment of the Lord is pure,
   enlightening the eyes;
9 the fear of the LORD is clean,
   enduring forever;
the rules[b] of the LORD are true,
   and righteous altogether.
10 More to be desired are they than gold,
   even much fine gold;
sweeter also than honey
   and drippings of the honeycomb.
11 Moreover, by them is your servant warned;
   in keeping them there is great reward.

Within these verses, the list states that we are to desire these truths and understand that they are far more valuable than money, goods, and wealth. It's way more precious than that. These scriptures describe the statutes, the commandments, the judgments, and the precepts—all of which mean the same thing: what God speaks to us. It is His instruction, His truth, His statements. If you follow these, what is the result? Your soul will be restored, you will have life, it will lead you to the best.

In the middle of the list is "the fear of the Lord." This also has the same meaning. The fear of the Lord is seeking and following His instruction. So, if you fear the Lord, what is your belief about His instruction? It's good, it's true, and it's more valuable than anything else. Does this mean you will have a full understanding of God's instruction when you first hear it? It is not likely.

In Acts 10, Peter was getting ready for dinner when he sees a vision of unclean animals. The Lord instructed him to rise up, kill it, and eat it. Did Peter immediately comply? No, he did not. In fact, he tells the Lord *no*. So, the Lord says it again, and again, Peter says *no*. When the Lord says it again and he says *no* for the third time, he begins to ponder it in his heart. Peter has fear of the Lord and seeks to follow God's instructions. He does not want to neglect it or ignore it. He knows there must be a truth there, but he just doesn't understand it yet. If Peter had chosen to ignore God's message, he wouldn't be fearing the Lord. He wouldn't have pursued it until he understood the meaning. Disregarding God's message clearly indicates that God is not being feared and that His words are not being taken as truth.

Where will you find God's truth? In Scripture. But even in Scripture you might come across things that don't make sense to you, things that are even contradictory. For example, Psalm 91 says, "If you abide in the shelter of the Almighty, no evil will befall you." But Jesus said there's trouble in the world, so how do you reconcile these two opposing statements? If you don't fear the Lord, you could leave it at that, saying that you guess it isn't true. If you fear the Lord, you take it the other direction. You stay with it and process it until you learn the truth about it. Fearing the Lord is believing with all certainty that His instruction is valuable, and it's absolutely true. You may not understand it, but you go after it, keep processing it, and stay with God until you do.

What are the benefits of fearing the Lord? What does that mean for how we then live it out? Why?

> **Read Psalm 25:12–15:**
>
> [12] Who is the man who fears the LORD?
>   Him will he instruct in the way that he should choose.
> [13] His soul shall abide in well-being,
>   and his offspring shall inherit the land.
> [14] The friendship[a] of the LORD is for those who fear him,
>   and he makes known to them his covenant.
> [15] My eyes are ever toward the LORD,
>   for he will pluck my feet out of the net.

____

____

____

____

____

If you fear the Lord, you believe that what He has to say is true even though you don't understand it yet. You do know that He will give you an abundant life, that He will tell you the secrets that you need to know to experience the abundant life. He will demonstrate to you His Covenant, which will drive you to listen and process because you believe what He has to say is going to matter. So, even though you don't understand it, you go after it, process it, and continue to seek wisdom.

LESSON 2: ABIDING, SPENDING TIME WITH HIM TO RECEIVE HIS HEART THAT BECOMES OUR HEART; WHAT NOT TO SPEAK AND WHAT WE ARE TO SPEAK.

When we are learning to receive God's direction in our lives, what is important for us to keep asking for? What does God promise when we ask for this? Why is this so important for us to understand as we walk this way?

Read James 1:5–8:

5 If any of you lacks wisdom, let him ask God, who gives generously to all without reproach, and it will be given him. 6 But let him ask in faith, with no doubting, for the one who doubts is like a wave of the sea that is driven and tossed by the wind. 7 For that person must not suppose that he will receive anything from the Lord; 8 he is a double-minded man, unstable in all his ways.

When do you lack wisdom? By definition, we lack wisdom all the time. We never know what awaits around the corner. We won't ever have the full picture. Things might look pretty good now, but only God knows what is ahead. Because we lack this wisdom, we should seek God so He can reveal which direction we should go. Listening to His guidance can actually prevent us from having adverse experiences. We need to listen to what He says instead of choosing our next step based upon what we might see. If we seek Him, He will provide the answer. In fact, if we seek Him, the only requirement is to believe that He will get the answer to us in a way that we will understand.

When our grandchildren were young, six- and nine-year-old brothers, they would stand in front of me and ask me the same question. When I gave my answer, the nine year old said, "I understand. No problem," while the six year old said, "I don't know what you are saying." Is it up to my six-year-old grandson to try to figure what I meant? Of course not. It is my responsibility to answer the question for him in a different way so that he understands.

LESSON 2: ABIDING, SPENDING TIME WITH HIM TO RECEIVE HIS HEART THAT BECOMES OUR HEART; WHAT NOT TO SPEAK AND WHAT WE ARE TO SPEAK.

When we have a heart to seek God and ask Him questions, He will get the answer to us in a way that we can understand it. That is His job, and He will deliver the answer every single time.

Even if you are a brand new believer and don't know anything about hearing the voice of the Holy Spirit, God says that if you have a heart to go and believe that He will give it to you, He absolutely will. If there is doubt or unbelief that He will provide answers to you, He won't. You have to believe with all certainty that when you go to God and ask Him for wisdom that He will answer you.

As we live out the Covenant, what are we to speak? What does that mean then to how we live things out? Why is this so important?

> **Read Proverbs 22:17–21:**
>
> Words of the Wise
>
> [17] Incline your ear, and hear the words of the wise,
>   and apply your heart to my knowledge,
> [18] for it will be pleasant if you keep them within you,
>   if all of them are ready on your lips.
> [19] That your trust may be in the LORD,
>   I have made them known to you today, even to you.
> [20] Have I not written for you thirty sayings
>   of counsel and knowledge,
> [21] to make you know what is right and true,
>   that you may give a true answer to those who sent you?

____

____

____

____

____

LESSON 2: ABIDING, SPENDING TIME WITH HIM TO RECEIVE HIS HEART THAT BECOMES OUR HEART; WHAT NOT TO SPEAK AND WHAT WE ARE TO SPEAK.

The Scripture is truly wonderful. Even if you think you are not skilled about hearing and receiving wisdom, God says He can still get it to us anyway. The critical piece of the process is to pay attention, incline your ear, listen. In doing this, you will learn to trust what you are hearing and will be able to share what you have learned. God's words will be on your lips. What does that mean? It means you can speak it because you have received it, understand it, and are able to share it. It's a beautiful circle: pay attention, hear it, receive it, understand it, and then speak it.

You are to stay with it until it is real to you and you can speak it. It can't be hypocritical. If you tell someone they should learn forgiveness but your life is in complete unforgiveness and hostility, how would you expect them to react? No one would take your words seriously. They would be hollow, empty, and have no meaning. If you invited someone to learn forgiveness, and they could see that you were living that way, they would have a better understanding of the benefit and value. They would be able to see that you are speaking the truth of what is inside you and that you are speaking out of your own experience.

In Romans 8:1-2, it says, "And so therefore, now there is no condemnation for those who are in Christ Jesus." If you pay attention and receive it, you will be able to speak it. In fact, over your lifetime, God is building the Library of Truth. Armed with this Library of Truth and the wisdom you've received and experienced, your speaking gets better and better and more profound.

Do not tell someone they should go and get forgiveness. Rather, ask them if they would like to learn forgiveness. If they are willing, work together, process together so they can learn how to receive it so they, too, can be transformed. Remember, in order for this to have any impact, make sure the words you speak are demonstrated in your life.

LESSON 2: ABIDING, SPENDING TIME WITH HIM TO RECEIVE HIS HEART THAT BECOMES OUR HEART; WHAT NOT TO SPEAK AND WHAT WE ARE TO SPEAK.

What is important about our heart and our intentions regarding how we live and speak? What does that mean for us? What are the consequences if we follow our own way? Why?

Read Proverbs 12:2; 5–6; 10; 13:

2 A good man obtains favor from the LORD,
    but a man of evil devices he condemns.
5 The thoughts of the righteous are just;
  the counsels of the wicked are deceitful.
6 The words of the wicked lie in wait for blood,
  but the mouth of the upright delivers them.
10 Whoever is righteous has regard for the life of his beast,
  but the mercy of the wicked is cruel.
13 An evil man is ensnared by the transgression of his lips,[a]
    but the righteous escapes from trouble.

____

____

____

____

____

For us to obtain favor and hear from God, we are to have a good heart, which is reflected in our intentions: Are you headed toward God or headed toward self? If you are headed toward Him, you will receive favor, but if you are headed toward self, you will be condemned.

What causes deceit? A different agenda. Instead of seeking God, it is purposely lying or spinning or covering up something for the sake of trying to get what you want. God said, "You're in a wicked place because your heart is deceitful, and you're speaking deceitfulness." How can you tell if you are walking with God? It is quite simple. If others are speaking deceit and you are walking with God, His Spirit within you will give you wisdom and will reveal the falsity of their words. In addition, you can share the truth—without judgment and hardness—and invite them to join you in that truth. Your role is to stay in the truth and the freedom of life with God.

What does cruel mean? Rolling over people with no regard to what they think, feel, or understand. Being mean without concern over their reaction. It is obvious when people are cruel and mean. God says, "The wicked will be snared or trapped by what they say." Getting caught in a snare usually happens when you are attracted to something, you pursue your own interest, and then you get caught in a trap that proved to be harmful or difficult. This is why what you say reflects your heart. You are either moving toward God and living in freedom or toward self and becoming trapped.

What is the impact of not telling the truth? What causes us not to tell the truth? When we fail to tell the truth, what do we bring upon ourselves? Why?

Read Mark 14:66–72:

Peter Denies Jesus

66 And as Peter was below in the courtyard, one of the servant girls of the high priest came, 67 and seeing Peter warming himself, she looked at him and said, "You also were with the Nazarene, Jesus." 68 But he denied it, saying, "I neither know nor understand what you mean." And he went out into the gateway[a] and the rooster crowed.[b] 69 And the servant girl saw him and began again to say to the bystanders, "This man is one of them." 70 But again he denied it. And after a little while the bystanders again said to Peter, "Certainly you are one of them, for you are a Galilean." 71 But he began to invoke a curse on himself and to swear, "I do not know this man of whom you speak." 72 And immediately the rooster crowed a second time. And Peter remembered how Jesus had said to him, "Before the rooster crows twice, you will deny me three times." And he broke down and wept.[c]

A girl comes to Peter with truth, "You know Jesus, don't you?" How does he respond? He says, "Absolutely not." He obviously knows this is truth, but he is lying. Why? He is lying out of fear because he is trying to protect himself. In doing this, what did he bring upon himself? He cursed himself. How did he curse himself? By denying the truth.

Keep this in mind as you are processing with your spouse or your inner circle when they say they see something or they would like you to understand something. You are called to process that truth. This does not necessarily mean that you are accepting it, just that you have a heart to process it with them. If you deny it and it's true, you're bringing what? Curses. Why? Because you have walked away from God. Instead of having a willingness to continue to process and ponder this new idea or new perspective by pursuing the truth, you are defensive and unwilling. This is a clear indicator that you have walked away from God. You have moved back into the flesh because what you said—your defensiveness and unwillingness—are both a reflection of your heart. The denial of the truth brings cursing, but pursuing the truth brings favor.

What do our words reveal? What does this mean for how we are to live and speak? Why?

Read Matthew 12:33–37:

A Tree Is Known by Its Fruit
[33] "Either make the tree good and its fruit good, or make the tree bad and its fruit bad, for the tree is known by its fruit. [34] You brood of vipers! How can you speak good, when you are evil? For out of the abundance of the heart the mouth speaks. [35] The good person out of his good treasure brings forth good, and the evil person out of his evil treasure brings forth evil. [36] I tell you, on the day of judgment people will give account for every careless word they speak, [37] for by your words you will be justified, and by your words you will be condemned."

Your words prove that you are either good or not good. Why? Because your words reveal your heart. Your words show the essence of the tree. Is there fruit there or not? Christ tells the Pharisees that what they say is illustrating their selfish desire to control others—as opposed to having a heart for their benefit to have them experience the Covenant. He tells them that even though they think the words they are speaking are good, the truth is they are not. Why? Because the words they were speaking were not His. His words are what is true, and the fruit of His words can easily be seen.

What does Christ tell us about being hypocritical? What does being hypocritical mean? Why is this so important to how we live?

Read Luke 6:37–45:

Judging Others

37 "Judge not, and you will not be judged; condemn not, and you will not be condemned; forgive, and you will be forgiven; 38 give, and it will be given to you. Good measure, pressed down, shaken together, running over, will be put into your lap. For with the measure you use it will be measured back to you."

39 He also told them a parable: "Can a blind man lead a blind man? Will they not both fall into a pit? 40 A disciple is not above his teacher, but everyone when he is fully trained will be like his teacher. 41 Why do you see the speck that is in your brother's eye, but do not notice the log that is in your own eye? 42 How can you say to your brother, 'Brother, let me take out the speck that is in your eye,' when you yourself do not see the log that is in your own eye? You hypocrite, first take the log out of your own eye, and then you will see clearly to take out the speck that is in your brother's eye.

A Tree and Its Fruit

43 "For no good tree bears bad fruit, nor again does a bad tree bear good fruit, 44 for each tree is known by its own fruit. For figs are not gathered from thornbushes, nor are grapes picked from a bramble bush. 45 The good person out of the good treasure of his heart produces good, and the evil person out of his evil treasure produces evil, for out of the abundance of the heart his mouth speaks.

____

____

____

____

____

Christ tells us not to be hypocritical by judging others. It's not your right to judge others. That's His privilege. Yes, there will be discernment, which we will cover in greater detail later, but that is far different than judging them and telling them what they should be doing or that you are right and they are wrong. Instead, invite them to the truth. Remember, it is good to speak truth because speaking truth is of Him.

If they reject that truth, are you to then go to judgment? No, that's not your responsibility. Your focus should be on dealing with your own issues, because everyone has plenty of their own issues to deal with. Don't worry about whether or not the truth is accepted, rather focus on the area in which God is asking you to grow.

The majority of the church is determined to correct those who don't agree with their position or beliefs. They are more than willing to make life miserable for others by coming against them, fighting them, arguing with them, even shunning them, if they deem it necessary. This is all done because of judgment. But, God says, "Don't go to judgment." That is His job, and He will deal with it in His way, in His timing.

LESSON 2: ABIDING, SPENDING TIME WITH HIM TO RECEIVE HIS HEART THAT BECOMES OUR HEART; WHAT NOT TO SPEAK AND WHAT WE ARE TO SPEAK.

As we learn to live His life, what are we to avoid? How do we tend to engage in these versus avoiding these? What are the consequences of not avoiding these, and what are the benefits of avoiding these? Why?

> **Read Titus 3:9–11:**
>
> [9] But avoid foolish controversies, genealogies, dissensions, and quarrels about the law, for they are unprofitable and worthless. [10] As for a person who stirs up division, after warning him once and then twice, have nothing more to do with him, [11] knowing that such a person is warped and sinful; he is self-condemned.

____

____

____

____

Verse 9 says to avoid foolish disputes. Disputes are of the flesh. Is that okay to have differing opinions? Of course. Not everyone will see things the exact same way. It's what you do with those different opinions that can lead to trouble. Do you immediately dispute and try to prove each other right or wrong? He said to avoid that. If you fall into that trap, it will drag you into the place of the enemy where instead of truth, you will be speaking death into them—as well as yourself. He said it's worthless. There's no value in that.

How often are we going to have disagreement and potential for dispute? All the time. Why? Because the world is full of self-centered people who are always working against us to judge us, oppose us, and run over us. This is true for people who are involved with our business, involved with ministry, involved with our family. They want to change you into something different or come against you, especially if they have power to really hurt you.

LESSON 2: ABIDING, SPENDING TIME WITH HIM TO RECEIVE HIS HEART THAT BECOMES OUR HEART; WHAT NOT TO SPEAK AND WHAT WE ARE TO SPEAK.

Keep in mind that a dispute is different than a disagreement. It's okay to disagree if we're willing to process truth. Dispute means you have established your truth, and you are not willing to be shown anything different. What is the result of holding this position? Foolishness and foolish disputes that never go anywhere. Why won't these disputes ever lead anywhere? Because you are seeking your will, your rules versus seeking God's will. When we've dug our heels in to stand our ground, we don't have a heart to process God's truth or receive His answers. This is worthless and is considered foolishness.

When the disciples were told to stop talking about the life of God, what was their response? Why did they respond this way? What was God telling them regarding how to talk about the life of God? Why?

Read Acts 4:13–20:

13 Now when they saw the boldness of Peter and John, and perceived that they were uneducated, common men, they were astonished. And they recognized that they had been with Jesus. 14 But seeing the man who was healed standing beside them, they had nothing to say in opposition. 15 But when they had commanded them to leave the council, they conferred with one another, 16 saying, "What shall we do with these men? For that a notable sign has been performed through them is evident to all the inhabitants of Jerusalem, and we cannot deny it. 17 But in order that it may spread no further among the people, let us warn them to speak no more to anyone in this name." 18 So they called them and charged them not to speak or teach at all in the name of Jesus. 19 But Peter and John answered them, "Whether it is right in the sight of God to listen to you rather than to God, you must judge, 20 for we cannot but speak of what we have seen and heard."

The disciples were told by the Sanhedrin to stop talking about Jesus publicly. How did they respond? They said they couldn't help but speak of what they had experienced. This is a big clue about what we are to speak. We are to fearlessly communicate what we have been experiencing. We are to speak of the reality of what is happening to us—which, if we are walking with God, will be reflecting His life in and around us. Never be afraid of that, and never let anybody silence those words. God reveals a key implication here: We are experiencing His supernatural work and learning His truths. Because we are living it out—experiencing it—we can speak it. However, if you are not living it out, do not speak about the life of God, but rather, focus on walking with Him so you may experience the life of God.

As God does supernatural things, especially overcoming the trouble that comes into our lives, what are we to do? How does that work? Why is this so important for our role in God's Kingdom?

Read Acts 5:17–20:

The Apostles Arrested and Freed
[17] But the high priest rose up, and all who were with him (that is, the party of the Sadducees), and filled with jealousy [18] they arrested the apostles and put them in the public prison. [19] But during the night an angel of the Lord opened the prison doors and brought them out, and said, [20] "Go and stand in the temple and speak to the people all the words of this Life."

____

____

____

____

____

Since the disciples did not stop speaking about the life of Jesus that they were experiencing, they were put in prison, but an angel breaks them out and frees them. What does the angel say to them? Stand out publicly and speak the life that they are experiencing. What's the reason for this instruction? Not to be defiant, but rather to tell those who have a heart to hear of the blessed life of Jesus and invite them to join them.

When you express the truth, others can observe the truth of your life because your life represents the truth. When you speak of the true life and power of the truth, they will listen. Don't be afraid to share it. Your life is to be receiving and speaking, receiving and speaking—bearing witness to that which leads to the Covenant. What does it mean if you are unable to speak this Covenant life? It means you are probably not experiencing it, and it is likely why you tend to go to the negative. It is why you tend to be harsh and go to grumbling. It is why you tend to get in disputes. The issue of what we speak reflects the true experience of our life.

When are we to speak, and when are we not to speak? What does this mean for how we know when to do either? Why?

> **Read Ecclesiastes 3:7:**
>
> [7] a time to tear, and a time to sew;
> a time to keep silence, and a time to speak;

____

____

____

____

____

There are seasons and times when we are called to speak and other times when we are called to be silent. Life with God is not a system—it is always relationship, and He will instruct us in the moments we are to be speaking and the moments we are to stay quiet. We are to simply follow His instruction.

When we are called to speak, what are we to speak? What exactly is this, and what is important for us to be able to speak this? Why?

Read Proverbs 8:1–9:

The Blessings of Wisdom
8 Does not wisdom call?
    Does not understanding raise her voice?
² On the heights beside the way,
    at the crossroads she takes her stand;
³ beside the gates in front of the town,
    at the entrance of the portals she cries aloud:
⁴ "To you, O men, I call,
    and my cry is to the children of man.
⁵ O simple ones, learn prudence;
    O fools, learn sense.
⁶ Hear, for I will speak noble things,
    and from my lips will come what is right,
⁷ for my mouth will utter truth;
    wickedness is an abomination to my lips.
⁸ All the words of my mouth are righteous;
    there is nothing twisted or crooked in them.
⁹ They are all straight to him who understands,
    and right to those who find knowledge.

____

____

____

____

____

When we speak, we are to speak wisdom, which comes from God. We are to go to Him with a heart to pursue and receive His wisdom, and we are to listen carefully, being certain His wisdom has been received before speaking the truth of what God is revealing.

What does it mean to turn from evil? How do we do this? What then does it mean to pursue peace (shalom)? How do we do this? Why are these two elements so important for how we live and thus how we speak?

Read Psalm 34:11–14:

¹¹ Come, O children, listen to me;
  I will teach you the fear of the LORD.
¹² What man is there who desires life
  and loves many days, that he may see good?
¹³ Keep your tongue from evil
  and your lips from speaking deceit.
¹⁴ Turn away from evil and do good;
  seek peace and pursue it.

____

____

____

____

____

We are to turn from evil. Remember, evil is defined as things that annoy, frustrate, irritate, oppress, and cause trouble. In other words, we don't need to put up with it. We may have experienced it, but we don't need to stay in that place and continue to put up with it. As we stand on this truth, what are we to pursue? Good, peace, shalom. Pursue what God is going to show you and reveal to you.

While pursuing what God is going to show you, don't speak evil: *This will never work. I'm never going to get out of this. I am never going to get a solution here. I'm going to be stuck with this. I guess this is God's will that I suffer and remain with this trouble.* That's speaking evil.

God says you don't need to put up with evil and to pursue peace. With a heart to follow God, ask Him what He has to say about the situation. In addition, His followers—the body of Christ—are to help each other hear what He has to say. Bring in your inner circle and ask them to process what God is revealing about the good and shalom that He promises. Together, pursue peace, shalom and turn from evil.

As we finish this lesson, we've learned that what we speak reflects what is in our heart. Are you willing to pursue God and seek Him, seek His wisdom, seek His Covenant life for you? Are you fearing the Lord and believing that what He has to say is true and that He will absolutely speak to you? Get His words on your lips so that what He says to you, you also can speak to others. Encourage each other to stay in that place of hearing and speaking. In doing this, God's power is stimulated. He will perform His good work, and you can facilitate it by what you say.

LESSON 3: HOW WE ARE TO LEARN TO SPEAK AS PROPHETS AND EXERCISE GOD'S AUTHORITY INTO OUR CIRCUMSTANCES AND INTO THE CIRCUMSTANCES OF OTHERS.

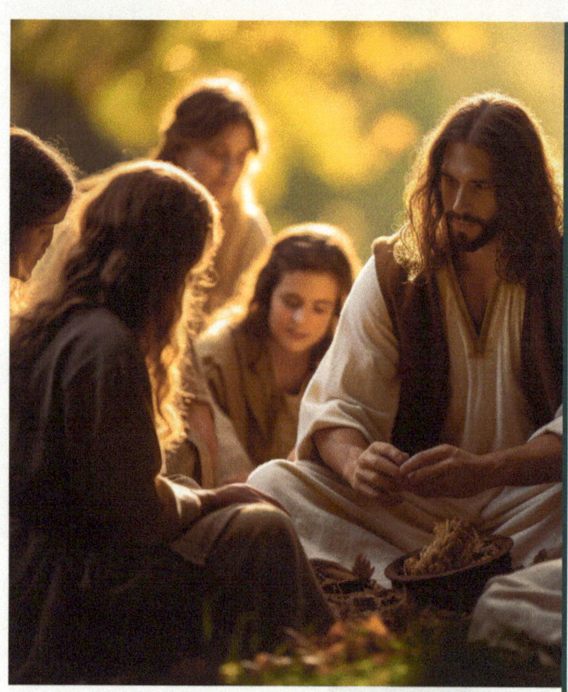

> **"The words we speak reflect what is in our heart, so what we speak tells the story of what we believe and what we have experienced."**

As we finish this course: *We Are What We Speak*, we have learned that the way we talk to each other is a reflection of what's inside of us—our beliefs. The words we speak reflect what is in our heart, so what we speak tells the story of what we believe and what we have experienced. We have learned that we are to continue to walk with God, learning the things of Him, and helping others around us—our spouse, friends, inner circle—also walk with God so they, too, can speak His words.

God encourages us to learn what it means to seek Him, to be with Him, to seek His wisdom, to walk with Him, and not to fall back into the flesh. Paul described our fundamental problems of the flesh: going to the negative, trying to figure things out yourself, and moving away from the life of God. What happens when you move away from the life of God? You put to death the life of the Spirit, and you're at enmity against God.

In the world, which is under the control of the Satan, we will have trouble. We are not exempt from that. Rather, life is about what we do with that trouble. Do we go to anger, bitterness, negativity, or complain and try to figure things out on our own, which usually results in a more adverse situation? Or, are we willing to let God resolve it because His way is always the Covenant? He promises He will deliver the Covenant to you. Stay with Him and let Him speak to you and give you the Covenant. Seek life and His will together with God through unity. Don't go to deceit and don't go to ignorance, but rather hear what He has to speak—which is His wisdom and understanding. As we continue, we will learn other elements of this life of God that we are to speak.

In what ways are we called to speak to others? What does this mean? How do we handle those who are considered weaker? What does it mean that they are weaker? Why is this so important for how we live and speak?

Read Romans 12:9–12; 16; 15:1–7:

Marks of the True Christian

9 Let love be genuine. Abhor what is evil; hold fast to what is good. 10 Love one another with brotherly affection. Outdo one another in showing honor. 11 Do not be slothful in zeal, be fervent in spirit,[a] serve the Lord. 12 Rejoice in hope, be patient in tribulation, be constant in prayer.

16 Live in harmony with one another. Do not be haughty, but associate with the lowly.[a] Never be wise in your own sight.

The Example of Christ

15 We who are strong have an obligation to bear with the failings of the weak, and not to please ourselves. 2 Let each of us please his neighbor for his good, to build him up. 3 For Christ did not please himself, but as it is written, "The reproaches of those who reproached you fell on me." 4 For whatever was written in former days was written for our instruction, that through endurance and through the encouragement of the Scriptures we might have hope. 5 May the God of endurance and encouragement grant you to live in such harmony with one another, in accord with Christ Jesus, 6 that together you may with one voice glorify the God and Father of our Lord Jesus Christ. 7 Therefore welcome one another as Christ has welcomed you, for the glory of God.

We are called to speak encouragement to others. The Greek word for encouragement goes deeper into its real meaning, which is *bringing harmony*. Within our community, our fellowship, we are to bring harmony and unity together with God through the Holy Spirit. We are to encourage each other to go to truth and seek God's will. We are to walk together with God as we understand all that we have learned. God's will begins with the Covenant.

If you have a problem, no matter how difficult or complicated, and you'd like to know how to process it and receive an answer, God calls us to be available for one another. We are to encourage each other with kindness, gentleness, and respect, offering to seek God and His will together. What happens when you seek God's will? You experience the Covenant. Our role is to speak true words of encouragement: *I understand. I know God has an answer. God's will is best and none better. Let's go find out. Let's go to harmony.* False encouragement (i.e., *Don't worry about it,* or *It'll be fine*) has no benefit.

The Covenant is also available for those who are considered weak. Why are they considered weak? Because they don't yet believe. They haven't experienced this yet, but if they have a heart to seek God and God's will, go with them. Come alongside them bringing encouragement with kindness, gentleness, and respect. Have patience, and don't expect the weaker person to be perfect and not to struggle with belief and understanding of how to receive God's answer. It takes practice, but we are to stay with them through that practice. Encourage them to continue as God will provide His answers that will lead to His will, which is best and none better. God will deliver His Covenant.

In what way are we to serve the body of Christ? For what purpose? How are we to carry this out in our Christian circles? Why is this so important?

Read 1 Corinthians 12:5–11:

5 and there are varieties of service, but the same Lord; 6 and there are varieties of activities, but it is the same God who empowers them all in everyone. 7 To each is given the manifestation of the Spirit for the common good. 8 For to one is given through the Spirit the utterance of wisdom, and to another the utterance of knowledge according to the same Spirit, 9 to another faith by the same Spirit, to another gifts of healing by the one Spirit, 10 to another the working of miracles, to another prophecy, to another the ability to distinguish

> between spirits, to another various kinds of tongues, to another the interpretation of tongues. [11] All these are empowered by one and the same Spirit, who apportions to each one individually as he wills.

____

____

____

____

____

This is always an interesting section because many believers have interpreted this to mean that each person is given a lifetime gift by the Spirit. This is not what these verses speak. Let's process this together. The verses say that we are to exercise faith. Well, we know something about faith. Hebrews 11:6 says, "Without faith, it's impossible to please God." We cannot say that since someone else was given the gift of faith, we are to go to them to believe for us. No. We all are called to live by faith, so it cannot be only a gift for some. Rather, God is teaching us about the manifestation at the moment. He is giving you a special anointing of the Holy Spirit to bring faith when you are speaking to somebody else. It is something He is giving you so that you can act on behalf of that other person.

If someone is struggling with believing, it doesn't mean they just need to rely on the faith of those who believe. Instead, we need to encourage that person to stay with God until they, too, believe. God gives us anointings in specific moments to bring into particular situations. It is a manifestation for this moment. It is giving us the exact gift in the exact moment so that we have exactly what we need to edify the body and further God's Kingdom.

God equips us to speak His truth and provide encouragement for others to go to Him, experience Him, see Him, and experience His will. All of us will experience God's gifts at various times. We speak these gifts, this spiritual understanding we are given in that moment, to encourage others not to quit, or to stay instead of walking way, not to go back to the flesh. We use the gift that was manifested for the moment to encourage them to stay in the Kingdom so God can deliver His Covenant.

What is the difference between speaking like a child and speaking with maturity? How do we then live and speak with maturity? Why is this so significant for how we live and speak?

Read 2 Corinthians 13:11–14:

Final Greetings

11 Finally, brothers,[a] rejoice. Aim for restoration, comfort one another,[b] agree with one another, live in peace; and the God of love and peace will be with you. 12 Greet one another with a holy kiss. 13 All the saints greet you.

14 The grace of the Lord Jesus Christ and the love of God and the fellowship of the Holy Spirit be with you all.

____

____

____

____

____

If you're mature, you don't speak like a child. How does a child speak? Out of ignorance. They speak ignorantly because they think they know something, but they really don't. They don't have the experience so they make assumptions. We are not to speak ignorantly. As we mature, we learn to speak truth based on what we've experienced through the life of the Spirit. The Spirit builds wisdom and understanding into each of us. If you have no experience with something or you haven't learned about it yet, do you have a right to speak about it? No. You can't truthfully speak about what you do not know. If someone tells you they are struggling with a certain issue and you have no knowledge of the issue, what may God be asking you to do? He just might be asking you to offer to go find out together what God has to say about it. Offer to learn this with them. Instead of speaking ignorantly as a child would, move together toward maturity. What we speak reflects that.

As we are called to build each other up, what are we called to do? What does this mean? How do we approach this when others do not have the same view we do? Why is this so important for our role in the body of Christ?

> **Read 2 Corinthians 13:11–14:**
>
> Final Greetings
> [11] Finally, brothers,[a] rejoice. Aim for restoration, comfort one another,[b] agree with one another, live in peace; and the God of love and peace will be with you. [12] Greet one another with a holy kiss. [13] All the saints greet you.
>
> [14] The grace of the Lord Jesus Christ and the love of God and the fellowship of the Holy Spirit be with you all.

____

____

____

____

____

What are you supposed to do for each other? Bring comfort and peace (shalom) by encouraging each other to go to oneness. Your words of encouragement are to stay together until you discover the fullness of God and receive wholeness. Why would you encourage a person to do that? Because this is where God commands blessing. There are important truths that we know about this: It doesn't do any good to get into foolish disputes. It doesn't do any good for one person to tell another person what they should do. Your role is not to chastise or tell them what to do, but rather for you to help them go to God's Word—to go together to see what the Word has to say. Do they have a heart to pursue God? It is really simple. If they do, then continue to bring encouragement, but if not, then move on—do not engage in foolish disputes. You do not have to persuade them of an answer because we know that the Word stands on its own. If they pursue God's Word, they will be in a position to react to it as the Spirit so leads them.

The subject of the rapture brings about serious discussion within the body of Christ. Many Christ followers say that the rapture is pre-trib, and they are certain of this because their church says it is certain. Because I have spent a considerable amount of time processing this from the Word, I can confidently tell them that they should not be so sure, but that we can go the Word together to see what God has to say about it. In the Word, there is no absoluteness as to whether the rapture will occur pre-trib, mid-trib, or post-trib. There are verses for all of those. But instead of telling them what I think they should believe, I invite them to look at it together. By going to the Word and seeking God's answers, they can come to their own conclusions.

There is also great debate over the issue of drinking. Some Christ followers say it is okay while others say it is absolutely not okay. But, instead of getting into disputes and ignorantly speaking like a child, offer to go to the Word together. In the Word, the issue of drinking is also not absolute. At times such as these, you need to process this with God and get this settled for you personally. God says He will give you wisdom about your life and situation. Since it's not absolute in the Word, He will give you clarity.

When there is great division among Christ followers on different issues, your role is to bring them to the Word. It is not your responsibility to determine whether what they are doing is good or not. If we go to the Word together, the Word will speak on its own. Your heart is to encourage each other to always go into the Word.

We are called to bear each other's burdens. What does that mean? How are we to speak in these situations? Why is this important for our role of helping each other?

Read Galatians 6:1–6:

Bear One Another's Burdens

6 Brothers,[a] if anyone is caught in any transgression, you who are spiritual should restore him in a spirit of gentleness. Keep watch on yourself, lest you too be tempted. [2] Bear one another's burdens, and so fulfill the law of Christ. [3] For if anyone thinks he is something, when he is nothing, he deceives himself. [4] But let each one test his own work, and then his reason to boast will be in himself alone and not in his neighbor. [5] For each will have to bear his own load.

[6] Let the one who is taught the word share all good things with the one who teaches.

Being a part of the body of Christ, we will observe sin, but remember, sin is rather simple. It is not walking with God, being in the flesh. What do these verses say we are to do when we witness this? Gently restore the person caught in a transgression back to what? Back to the relationship—back to walking with God. Telling them they better stop what they are doing or they need to change or fix things in their life is not gently restoring them back to the relationship with God.

There are a number of executives I disciple who have a problem with pornography. They are trapped in it, very active in it, have tried to stop it, but they can't. Each of them believes their sin is the act of watching pornography. But, it's not. The sin is that they are not walking with God to be healed from this. If I were to tell them to stop it, my words would be useless. They have tried, but it didn't work. In the flesh, you just can't do it.

Instead, I ask them if they want to be healed of this addiction. Generally, they really do, because they know it's oppressive and a heavy burden in their life. The best thing I can do for them is to help them go to God, walk together with them so they can walk with Him in His Kingdom, and abide in the Word which will bring healing and restoration from their addiction. If they do, we know that God will bring real healing and restoration. This is how we bear each other's burdens.

So, rather than being judgmental toward people caught in pornography or any number of other things that take them away from God, what should our heart be? To encourage them to the life of God. Help them get to the Lord by bearing their burdens and walking with them. There's no judgement in your words, only an invitation to the wonderful Covenant life of God. These are the same words God would speak because His heart is to provide restoration and healing.

As we are called to hear, receive, and follow God's will, how are we to assist others in the same for their lives? On what basis can we be assured we will reach understanding of God's will? Why is this so important regarding how we process and speak?

Read Ephesians 4:1–6:

Unity in the Body of Christ

4 I therefore, a prisoner for the Lord, urge you to walk in a manner worthy of the calling to which you have been called, [2] with all humility and gentleness, with patience, bearing with one another in love, [3] eager to maintain the unity of the Spirit in the bond of peace. [4] There is one body and one Spirit—just as you were called to the one hope that belongs to your call— [5] one Lord, one faith, one baptism, [6] one God and Father of all, who is over all and through all and in all.

This tells us to work really, really, really hard, with respect and honor, to go to the unity of the Spirit to discover God's will because this is where He's going to command blessing and the Covenant will be known. Work really, really hard with honor and respect and encourage others to seek God's will together. Stay together until you reach unity, which is the understanding of God's will in the Spirit. It's a step-by-step process. Even if we think we have the answer, it is not ours to give. Rather, walk with God who says, *Walk with Me. Go step by step with Me—I'll give you truth, and I'll help you understand it.*

Why can we be assured of this? Because the Spirit is one. And we believers all have the same Holy Spirit who is one. He can't tell us two different things. So, if, together, we work hard to seek the unity of the Spirit, we will receive it. In doing this, we will discover God's will—which is best and none better.

As we are in process seeking God's will together, what is critical for us to understand about what we speak? What does that mean? Why is this such an important part of the process?

Read Ephesians 4:25–26:

[25] Therefore, having put away falsehood, let each one of you speak the truth with his neighbor, for we are members one of another. [26] Be angry and do not sin; do not let the sun go down on your anger,

---

In the simplest of terms, this says, "Don't lie to each other." This is interesting because it is not talking about deceiving each other. Rather, in what way do people tend to lie to one another? By not speaking their truth, by keeping quiet when they know something. God says that lying is actually being silent when you know something.

We have learned that we are to encourage others to pursue God with the truth and speak our truth to them. Our truth is not necessarily absolute truth as it is our perspective, our personal insight on this particular issue. But with a heart to seek God's truth together, we can each speak our personal truth, and as we process this, we will be led to God's truth—the unity of the Spirit.

In order to ensure that the devil doesn't draw us away into contention and debate and judgment, we need to encourage each other. God will show us His absolute truth when we seek Him. The best thing we can do is to help one another see God's truth.

Recently, I was in a conversation with a group that I'm discipling. One lady, in particular, is trying to discover a new path. She's in a certain place in business, and she recognizes that she is not supposed to be there. She knows that she needs to go somewhere else, and she's processing it. I shared with her the analogy that God is putting together a jigsaw puzzle. While we would just like the answer, God says He will give us the answer piece by piece, and we are to trust that He will connect the pieces so that we will then see the answer.

When I asked her how it was going, she said that there were certain things that she believed were not what she was supposed to do, and there were a few things that she felt she should pursue. I asked her what she was doing with those options, and she said she didn't know if she should still pursue all of them—including the ones she knew weren't right for her. I asked her, "What's the truth? What have you heard?" I then told her to receive that, and stand on that truth, to move forward on what she knew, and trust that God was leading her. If, for some reason, we miss something, do not fret, He will bring it back to us to process.

This is how it works. We facilitate the process by speaking truth and helping others stand on the truth of what they are receiving, and we bring encouragement to trust the work of the Holy Spirit as He leads us to His will.

As we continue to learn the process, describe what we are to do and what God is doing. What then does that mean is our new definition of prayer? How does this work, and how does this benefit us? Why is this so important for us in seeking and speaking His will?

Read Malachi 3:16–18:

The Book of Remembrance

[16] Then those who feared the LORD spoke with one another. The Lord paid attention and heard them, and a book of remembrance was written before him of those who feared the LORD and esteemed his name. [17] "They shall be mine, says the LORD of hosts, in the day when I make up my treasured possession, and I will spare them as a man spares his son who serves him. [18] Then once more you shall see the distinction between the righteous and the wicked, between one who serves God and one who does not serve him.

As we are seeking God's will together, the best thing we can do is talk to each other. While we are talking and processing, who is listening? God. He then gives us wisdom, insight, and clarity so that we can discern the truth between good and evil. So, when we are talking to each other, what are we actually doing? Praying. God is listening to our conversations.

As we speak and ask each other questions, God provides insight and instruction for us to bring encouragement. God hears our words, responds, and brings wisdom and revelation.

I attended a group where a Christian business person presented his company review. During his presentation, he made a statement and then continued on with his review. I stopped him and asked if he heard what he had just said. When he repeated what he had said, everyone in the room realized how significant this was. We knew it was insight from God and was a piece of the resolution for a key issue in his company. All we were doing was talking to each other—which also implies listening to each other—and the Holy Spirit spoke to help him to understand the significance of his words.

What are the definitions of prophetic? How are we to engage in this gifting? What are the qualities of prophetic? Why is this so critical in our helping each other hear, receive, and follow God's will?

> **Read 1 Corinthians 14:1–3:**
>
> Prophecy and Tongues
> **14** Pursue love, and earnestly desire the spiritual gifts, especially that you may prophesy. [2] For one who speaks in a tongue speaks not to men but to God; for no one understands him, but he utters mysteries in the Spirit. [3] On the other hand, the one who prophesies speaks to people for their upbuilding and encouragement and consolation.

____

____

____

____

____

LESSON 3: HOW WE ARE TO LEARN TO SPEAK AS PROPHETS AND EXERCISE GOD'S AUTHORITY INTO OUR CIRCUMSTANCES AND INTO THE CIRCUMSTANCES OF OTHERS.

There are two forms of prophetic.

1. Foretelling. Having insight about what God is up to and knowing that we are to pay attention to what is coming ahead. Being able to foretell something that needs to be pursued. Basically, it is a head's up from God.

2. Forthtelling. Telling the truth about a situation and giving insight into what God is saying about the situation. This should only be done after being invited into the process and being given permission to speak into the situation.

Is it our burden to worry about speaking into every issue or situation we learn of or witness? No. In addition, when we have been given the truth, we need to ask God if He wants us to share this truth, intercede, pray they receive the truth, or say something. If God wants us to speak His truth, He will guide us to do so. It is not our responsibility to tell somebody the truth we have received, rather, it is our responsibility to follow God regarding what He is asking us to do when we are called into this prophetic role.

What are the three qualities, or characteristics, of a prophetic role?

1. Encouragement—God is speaking His wonderful will and He has given you a piece of this to provide encouragement for others to stay with it, to receive it, and have clarity of the steps into His will.

2. Comfort—this word from God is to bring hope, adventure, a path to resolution of your trouble or problem or decision.

3. Admonishment—this ranges from instruction regarding steps to take to walk on His path to warning a person who is walking the wrong way and needs to repent, turn around, and return to the Kingdom to receive God's will.

Each of these qualities must be handled with respect and kindness. God will give us the courage to speak the truth—what God is revealing to me—if speaking the truth is His will. If He leads us to issue a warning to someone, we can relay that we can't confirm what they are doing and urge them to reconsider, to go back to God and pursue Him and His will. Offer to help them do just that. The role of the prophetic is to encourage and comfort and admonish, and God's prophetic word is to lift you up to get you to the Kingdom. This all goes hand in hand with our call to be a watchman.

From the following two sets of verses: As we go deeper into the prophetic, what is the role of a watchman? How does it work? What is important for us to understand about this role—the consequences of following or deciding not to follow? What, then, is crucial for us to be able to carry out the assignment?

Read Ezekiel 2:1–8:

Ezekiel's Call

2 And he said to me, "Son of man,[a] stand on your feet, and I will speak with you." [2] And as he spoke to me, the Spirit entered into me and set me on my feet, and I heard him speaking to me. [3] And he said to me, "Son of man, I send you to the people of Israel, to nations of rebels, who have rebelled against me. They and their fathers have transgressed against me to this very day. [4] The descendants also are impudent and stubborn: I send you to them, and you shall say to them, 'Thus says the LORD GOD.' [5] And whether they hear or refuse to hear (for they are a rebellious house) they will know that a prophet has been among them. [6] And you, son of man, be not afraid of them, nor be afraid of their words, though briers and thorns are with you and you sit on scorpions.[b] Be not afraid of their words, nor be dismayed at their looks, for they are a rebellious house. [7] And you shall speak my words to them, whether they hear or refuse to hear, for they are a rebellious house.

[8] "But you, son of man, hear what I say to you. Be not rebellious like that rebellious house; open your mouth and eat what I give you."

____

____

____

____

____

As we are called into the role of the watchman, into the role of the prophetic, we are to speak only what? Truth—what He tells us. We are to only speak what He tells us. Don't be afraid, just speak what He tells you. Does it matter whether they receive it or not? No. Is that your job? No. It is not your job to persuade them, only to share God's message with them.

LESSON 3: HOW WE ARE TO LEARN TO SPEAK AS PROPHETS AND EXERCISE GOD'S AUTHORITY INTO OUR CIRCUMSTANCES AND INTO THE CIRCUMSTANCES OF OTHERS.

Read Ezekiel 3:16–27:

A Watchman for Israel

16 And at the end of seven days, the word of the Lord came to me: 17 "Son of man, I have made you a watchman for the house of Israel. Whenever you hear a word from my mouth, you shall give them warning from me. 18 If I say to the wicked, 'You shall surely die,' and you give him no warning, nor speak to warn the wicked from his wicked way, in order to save his life, that wicked person shall die for[a] his iniquity, but his blood I will require at your hand. 19 But if you warn the wicked, and he does not turn from his wickedness, or from his wicked way, he shall die for his iniquity, but you will have delivered your soul. 20 Again, if a righteous person turns from his righteousness and commits injustice, and I lay a stumbling block before him, he shall die. Because you have not warned him, he shall die for his sin, and his righteous deeds that he has done shall not be remembered, but his blood I will require at your hand. 21 But if you warn the righteous person not to sin, and he does not sin, he shall surely live, because he took warning, and you will have delivered your soul."

22 And the hand of the LORD was upon me there. And he said to me, "Arise, go out into the valley,[b] and there I will speak with you." 23 So I arose and went out into the valley, and behold, the glory of the LORD stood there, like the glory that I had seen by the Chebar canal, and I fell on my face. 24 But the Spirit entered into me and set me on my feet, and he spoke with me and said to me, "Go, shut yourself within your house. 25 And you, O son of man, behold, cords will be placed upon you, and you shall be bound with them, so that you cannot go out among the people. 26 And I will make your tongue cling to the roof of your mouth, so that you shall be mute and unable to reprove them, for they are a rebellious house. 27 But when I speak with you, I will open your mouth, and you shall say to them, 'Thus says the Lord GOD.' He who will hear, let him hear; and he who will refuse to hear, let him refuse, for they are a rebellious house.

God says He is calling you to speak to others in the body of Christ. This scripture explains that when God leads you to speak to others in the body, it can include warnings to invite back those who have walked away from Him. He will instruct you on what to say, who to say it to, and when to say it. What are you to do? Follow His instruction.

If you follow His instruction and are faithful, speaking His word with kindness, respect, and honor, you will be blessed. God's truth stands on its own, and the ball is in their court to respond to the warning. If you do not follow His instruction, you are being disobedient, and the consequences are on you. You are God's sheepdog, His watchman. They may or may not accept His word to them, but for you, it doesn't matter. Don't look at the outcome. You are not called to persuade them in any way, rather to deliver His warning to invite them back to the Covenant life. This is always the heart of God.

If we are abiding as Christ has revealed to us, how are we to pray and thus speak? What does this mean regarding the process of abiding and then praying? Why is this so important to our receiving the promises of God through our prayer life?

Read John 15:7–8:

[7] If you abide in me, and my words abide in you, ask whatever you wish, and it will be done for you. [8] By this my Father is glorified, that you bear much fruit and so prove to be my disciples.

If you are abiding in the vine, in the relationship of Christ, and remain connected to this life, and His words abide in you—you have heard, received, and believe that He has spoken personally to you—His rhema words. What can you do with this? You can pray it and speak it, and by this entire process of abiding, the Father will perform what He has spoken. Why? Because you have discovered His will, and He promises to fulfill it. By this, the Father is glorified. How? Through changed circumstances—fruit. Your role is to stay with Him all the way through the process. Are these words abiding in you? Do you understand it? Do you believe it? As you pray it and speak it, it will be so—Amen. You are bringing authority, the power of God, to the situation by speaking the message He gave you.

As we learned about abiding, if we pray according to His will, what does that mean God must do? In addition, what must we do? Why is speaking so critical to the process? What then can we expect as we follow this process?

Read 1 John 5:14–15:

[14] And this is the confidence that we have toward him, that if we ask anything according to his will he hears us. [15] And if we know that he hears us in whatever we ask, we know that we have the requests that we have asked of him.

Your prayer life is going to facilitate God fulfilling His will for you. You are to pray according to His will. This is not us guessing His will or telling God what you desire for Him to do for you. You are to stay in process until you know God's will. He is listening to confirm that you know His will because you can speak it—and then He will fulfill it. If you are not quite there yet, He will keep you in process until you have full understanding. Your role is to stay in process and help others stay in process until God's will is known and clear.

As we are learning how to hear, receive, and follow God's will, what privilege does God give us to confirm and know His will? How then does this work practically for us? What power does this bring to us in our situations? Why?

> **Read Matthew 18:18–20:**
>
> [18] Truly, I say to you, whatever you bind on earth shall be bound in heaven, and whatever you loose on earth shall be loosed[a] in heaven. [19] Again I say to you, if two of you agree on earth about anything they ask, it will be done for them by my Father in heaven. [20] For where two or three are gathered in my name, there am I among them."

____

____

____

____

____

Where two or three are gathered in Christ's name, what are you seeking? His will. We are to gather together—with your spouse, with a friend, with a group, to hear His answer and resolve this issue for you. It is finding out together—in unity and harmony with the Holy Spirit—what His will is. The processing and discussing takes time as it is a step-by-step process. In addition, the reality of free will and differing opinions oftentimes causes delays. Does this mean that God's will won't come to fruition? Absolutely not. It means He has another path that should be followed. He is sovereign and can make all things work for our good. Nothing is too hard for Him.

When we reach agreement and receive and believe His will, we can speak it and bring authority and power to our situations—which is the ability to bind off the power of the enemy and loose the power of heaven into this circumstance. We discovered His will together, and are now going to pray it and speak it, and it will be done.

As we grow in our prayer life through abiding and understanding God's will, what are we called to speak to? What does that mean? How does this work practically for us? What is also important regarding the issue of unforgiveness? Why?

Read Mark 11:20–25:

The Lesson from the Withered Fig Tree

[20] As they passed by in the morning, they saw the fig tree withered away to its roots. [21] And Peter remembered and said to him, "Rabbi, look! The fig tree that you cursed has withered." [22] And Jesus answered them, "Have faith in God. [23] Truly, I say to you, whoever says to this mountain, 'Be taken up and thrown into the sea,' and does not doubt in his heart, but believes that what he says will come to pass, it will be done for him. [24] Therefore I tell you, whatever you ask in prayer, believe that you have received[a] it, and it will be yours. [25] And whenever you stand praying, forgive, if you have anything against anyone, so that your Father also who is in heaven may forgive you your trespasses."[b]

____

____

____

____

____

There's great authority here. The story is about Jesus on Palm Sunday and how He curses a tree as He walks into Jerusalem. The next day, they are walking back out to Bethany, and Peter points out that the tree had withered up.

Jesus was glad they noticed and used the opportunity to reveal something about their prayer life. The Bible says to have faith in God, but the Greek translation more precisely says to have the faith OF God. God is the author and finisher of faith, and He will give it to you when you believe it.

He adds an important truth to this process. If you're praying and learning this process of powerful prayer and He shows that you have unforgiveness in your heart toward somebody, what are you supposed to do? Get that resolved first. Your prayer will not be answered until you get this resolved, because you don't care about this person as He does. It is important to understand that it doesn't say you need to reconcile or go get things settled, it means your heart is free of the heaviness of the offense. You have given them forgiveness and are demonstrating His nature is operating in you.

Jesus discussed the mountain in front of you. Yes, it's a problem. It's an issue. And, there are things that are causing you trouble. So, what are you supposed to do? Speak to the mountain. Speak what? His will, His truth, and His authority. You aren't to pray that God takes care of the mountain, instead, you are to speak directly to that specific mountain. *This is going to stop! This is going to change! This is going to be fulfilled by what God has spoken to me!* You have received the faith of God to speak it because you know it to be true.

Verse 24 says, "Therefore, I tell you, whatever you ask in prayer, believe that you have received it, and it shall be done." Why? Because God sees it done already. It's finished and completed. He says to join Him and see what He knows. You are also to believe it's already done. When it is all based on faith, you can speak it, and it will be done in time.

When can you speak God's promise out loud to other people? When you believe it and know it because you see what God sees. If you aren't sure, are you going to have the confidence that you can speak it? No. This lack of confidence means that you didn't go far enough. You—and your spouse and inner circle—didn't reach the place of unity and harmony with the Holy Spirit where you are certain that what you know is absolute. Ask yourself these questions: Do I understand this? Can I speak it? Do I believe His will? Do I have confidence that what God has spoken to me will happen and that I can speak it out?

In the story of the centurion in Matthew 8, the centurion asked Jesus if He could come and heal his servant who was really sick and suffering. Jesus agrees to do this. Then, the centurion tells Jesus that He doesn't need to bother to physically go to his servant because all Jesus needed to do was say the word. The centurion was a leader with authority, and when he spoke, his men followed. He noticed this with Jesus also. When Jesus spoke, things happened. He knew that Jesus' words brought about the power.

It's not a magical thing, and it is not a mechanical thing that you can speak things on your own. Rather, it is based upon what you have heard from God and then speak into the situation. We have described this as faith—based upon what you've heard, received, and then can speak. Further, we speak to each other to be encouraged to stay in process until we are certain we know God's will and can bring God's authority.

As we are called to teach others what we are learning, what does it mean that we are God's fragrance? What does that mean? How will others react to us being God's fragrance, and how should we respond to these reactions? Why is this so important in our role of serving the body?

Read 2 Corinthians 2:14–3:6:

14 But thanks be to God, who in Christ always leads us in triumphal procession, and through us spreads the fragrance of the knowledge of him everywhere. 15 For we are the aroma of Christ to God among those who are being saved and among those who are perishing, 16 to one a fragrance from death to death, to the other a fragrance from life to life. Who is sufficient for these things? 17 For we are not, like so many, peddlers of God's word, but as men of sincerity, as commissioned by God, in the sight of God we speak in Christ.

Ministers of the New Covenant

3 Are we beginning to commend ourselves again? Or do we need, as some do, letters of recommendation to you, or from you? 2 You yourselves are our letter of recommendation, written on our[a] hearts, to be known and read by all. 3 And you show that you are a letter from Christ delivered by us, written not with ink but with the Spirit of the living God, not on tablets of stone but on tablets of human hearts.[b]

4 Such is the confidence that we have through Christ toward God. 5 Not that we are sufficient in ourselves to claim anything as coming from us, but our sufficiency is from God, 6 who has made us sufficient to be ministers of a new covenant, not of the letter but of the Spirit. For the letter kills, but the Spirit gives life.

These verses describe our role as a minister, which is to discover God's will and then help others also discover God's will. As a minister, you are to bring life. What kind of life? Super-abundant life, Covenant life. That's the purpose of ministry. Bring the life. He says two things about this:

1. You're a beautiful fragrance.

2. This beautiful fragrance brings either life or death.

Some willingly receive it and experience life. Others who do not have a heart to receive it, reject it and experience death. What did you bring? The opportunity to be the fragrance of the Covenant. The opportunity is not given out of judgment—it is just the invitation to the life of God. So, the purpose of this is to speak to others about the life we are experiencing ourselves. It is about their heart, not yours. Is it your responsibility to chase them down and persuade them? No, God alone bears that burden. Rather, we are to go where God leads.

There is additional good news. The sufficiency and competency for being this fragrance is based solely on the life of God in you. It is not reserved only for the talented and skilled. It is available to everyone. Therefore, can we have the same powerful ministry that Billy Graham had? Yes. Is it dependent on how skilled we are? No, because the competency is whose? God's, and all we have to do is what? Just be with Him. He will freely give you this ministry of the fragrance of offering the abundant life.

How do we approach this? If we look at this life of having to be perfect and follow the Bible as law, what happens? It kills. It will kill off any power of the life in the Spirit, and you will have no ability to be the wonderful fragrance. But if you approach it as life, it brings the abundant life.

If it is your role to bring others to the Covenant, you must then stay in the Covenant. But keep in mind that we do not stay in the Covenant in isolation. What do we need from each other? Encouragement to stay in the Covenant, to understand what God's will is.

Do you want to experience the life of God? This is our ministry. Even though someone is discouraged, upset, angry, frustrated, or facing awful things, your role as a sufficient minister is to go to God together and seek His will, which is the Covenant for all of our situations. This is why speaking is so critical.

We can either live in the Covenant, enjoying the super-abundant life, or we can go back to the trouble of the world and struggle. It's all about what you believe and then what you say. It's about leading others to truth and walking together to speak life.

As we end this course, we encourage you to spend more time learning these truths. Pay attention to what you're saying. It is reflective of you walking with God and your life with God. It is the Covenant, learning to go to the Covenant, and encouraging others to live in the Covenant. Learn the importance of speaking, which is reflective of your heart. Let God give you a heart of joy and freedom and purpose so that you may speak His truth and help others receive His life, receive a changed heart, and live out the Covenant life.

living waters
Abide™
MINISTRIES

History of
Abide Ministries

In the 1990s, Rich and Linda Case received a call from God to dig into what it means to truly live in the Spirit.

In the 1990s, Rich and Linda Case received a call from God to dig into what it means to truly live in the Spirit. They had been believers for most of their lives and regularly attended church and Bible studies, but began to realize that, despite knowing the Bible intellectually, their personal experiences seemed disconnected from the promises and truths found in scripture. As they then learned these essential truths through their abiding and hearing God's voice — and began to see the grand life play out in their lives God called them to give that knowledge away. In 2001, God initiated the ABIDE ministry at a retreat with friends in Austria, and through their personal experience of this abiding life, their friends noticed the change in their lives and inquired if Rich and Linda could host a similar retreat the following year. This was repeated three years in a row, and then God called them to host weekend retreats in their home in Colorado.

Through the formal development of the truths revealed by God with Abiding and additional electives, they founded All for Jesus — Living Waters Ministries, now Abide Ministries — and have seen it grow exponentially since then, with 24+ retreat leaders all over the world, 29 online courses, eight books on various aspects of living life with Christ, and a daily podcast. Rich and Linda have also worked with various churches to strengthening them with the truths of an abiding life in Christ, and seeing Christ bring reconciliation and new vision to desperate situations.

Their heart is to bring the truths and promises of God to as many people as possible, showing everyone that when you abide in Christ and seek Him daily, your life can be completely and utterly transformed — enabling you to experience the grand life promised by God.

Vision

At our core, we believe in walking along God's path and connecting to the vine (abiding). As we walk in unity with others and understand God's Word as the truth, we are sure to experience His promised grand life and thus, willingly accept God's will as our chosen path.

Mission

1. Live out and invite everyone to experience the grand, spectacular, abundant life by hearing God's voice.
2. Share God's majesty, a close relationship with us as he yearns for our restoration.
3. God is majestic, grand and pure goodness, so that we can experience His nature in real life.
4. Communicate to everyone, irrespective of their condition, that all are meant to experience God's Divine Life (grand, majestic), by receiving His personal plan for us.
5. God delivers this life for us in a SUPERNATURAL way, transcending human comprehension, and thus, becoming normal in our life.
6. Teach that personal truths are revealed to us by God, grounded on His word – the embodiment of Truth.
7. Recognize that abiding in Christ changes our life in tangible, real ways, and is not just learning about or studying this life.
8. Teach that as we abide in Christ, we learn to understand and amp; follow God's will for our lives, as He leads us personally into His grand, Divine plan for us. His personal plan calls us into His bigger story with our best interest at heart (blessed to bless others).

Testimonies

"If I'm not abiding, I feel like I'm dying. Abiding is living…It's powerful to know that you have God's perspective on something."

 **Steve**

"This was the first time that I understood what people meant by God's living Word. And I've been a Christian for a lot of years, but this was the first time it really came alive for me and I really could experience that."

 **Dan**

"It doesn't matter where you are at in your walk. If you just got saved yesterday or if you've been a 20+ year believer like i have, learning how to hear God's voice and learning His will is just as important in day one as it is in day 3,426. You wanna hear God's will and this course has helped me hear Him more clearly."

 **Bob**

"Abiding turned out to be the most transformational thing I've ever had since salvation in my Christian walk and in our marriage, and it's just been amazing. God has a path for us and He is there and He's showing it to us."

 **Heath**

"Before, in my quiet time, it was more of a checklist thing for me to do in the morning, and, honestly, some mornings it was the thing that went if I was busy, and some days it didn't even happen. Now, it's become so personal to me and the time flies by in the morning and God speaks so directly to me and I just never felt that way on a daily basis before. That has been life-altering for me."

 **Rebecca**

"I heard about people living in peace, I heard about people living in joy, and realizing all kinds of things around them are happening. And then we realize, wait a minute, we're there, we have peace beyond understanding."

 **Brad**

Giving to the Ministry

Have you experienced abundant blessing from your time with Abide Ministries?

Pay it forward by donating at **abideministries.com/donate** and help us support others in learning how to seek Christ and abide in Him! We appreciate your desire to help us share the Abundant Life with the rest of the world.

Learn More at
abideministries.com

Podcast

Escape the chaos and uncertainty of the world with our podcast, *"Come and See, Finding Truth in a World of Chaos,"* available on YouTube, Apple Podcasts, and Spotify.

CHANNEL   PLAYLIST PAGE

Tune in five days a week as our hosts, Rich Case and Kathy Rocconi, dive into the scriptures and discuss what it looks like to live an abiding life with Christ. Join us as we seek God's truth in a world of turmoil and darkness.

Online
Courses

Abide Ministries online courses uncover life-changing biblical truths, with practical application and wisdom. Our courses are joyful and life-giving and are perfect for small groups as well as individuals.

Each course has an accompanying workbook. Join us as we learn about biblical topics like Hearing God's Voice, Discerning God's Will, the Covenant, Living in Forgiveness, Living in the Kingdom of God, Living in the Supernatural, Christ, Clutter and the Calendar, Living the Grand Life, and many, many more.

COURSES

Abide
Retreats

Learn more at
abideministries.com

Do you have friends or a small group that you would like to experience what you just experienced?

Would you be interested in attending another retreat, which we call electives to go deeper in your walk with God?

See the various options on our website.
The topics for retreats and courses are the same.